Shenandoah

Thanks Dave,

H.

Shenandoah

Daughter of the Stars

Photographs by Lucian Niemeyer   Text by Julia Davis

LOUISIANA STATE UNIVERSITY PRESS *Baton Rouge & London*

Lucian, Michelle, and Heather—

each of you has had experiences of

value in the Shenandoah

Copyright © 1945, 1994 by Julia Davis (text) and © 1994 by Lucian Niemeyer
(photographs, Preface, and Epilogue)

All rights reserved

Manufactured in China

First printing

03   02   01   00   99   98   97   96   95   94   5 4 3 2 1

Typeface: Aldus

Typesetter: G&S Typesetters, Inc.

Printer and binder: Toppan Printing Co. , Inc.

Library of Congress Cataloging-in-Publication Data

Niemeyer, Lucian.

Shenandoah : daughter of the stars / photographs by Lucian
Niemeyer ; text by Julia Davis.

p.   cm.

Includes index.

ISBN 0-8071-1966-0

1. Shenandoah River Valley (Va. and W. Va.)—Pictorial works.
2. Shenandoah River Valley (Va. and W. Va.)—History.   I. Davis,
Julia, 1900–1993.   II. Title.

F232.S5N54   1994

975.5'9—dc20   94-18981

                                                             CIP

Contents

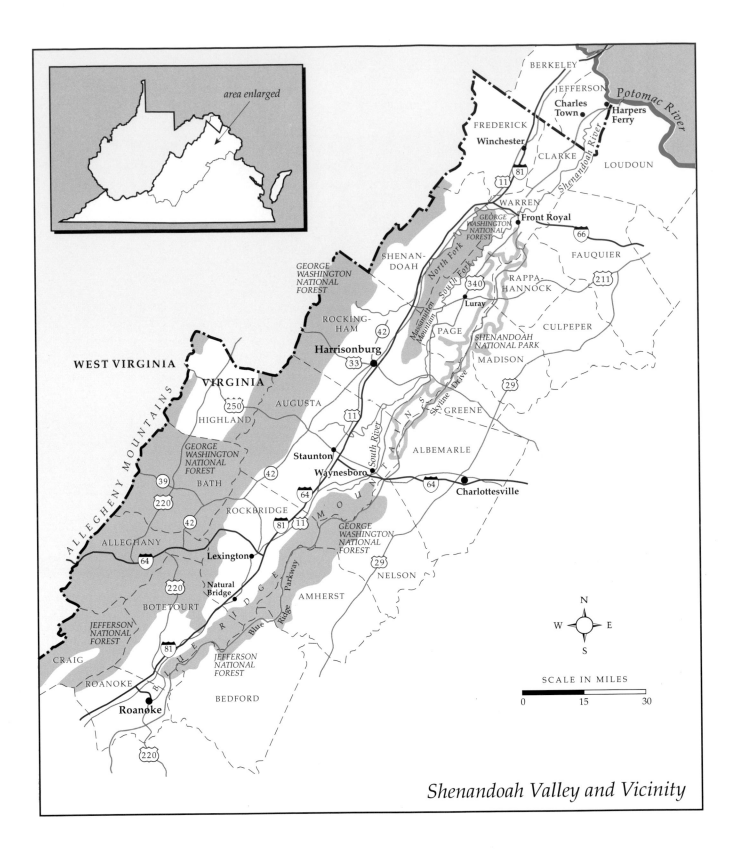

Shenandoah Valley and Vicinity

Preface

Shenandoah is music. It harmonizes easily in my soul. It inspires peace in me even when I am not there, peace that increases greatly when I am there. It blesses me. Though I am not a Valley native, my memories are etched with experiences there for over forty years. I have been enriched by its bountiful natural order. From mountains to valleys and then to rivers and haze, it is an old, gentle land with the soft resonance of long human living.

Technically, the Shenandoah Valley is the watershed of the Shenandoah River, which has its southernmost source near Steeles Tavern and, fed by myriad mountain streams, flows northeast between the Blue Ridge and the Alleghenies to Front Royal, where the river's North and South Forks unite before rolling on to empty into the Potomac at Harpers Ferry. (Because the river runs more or less northward, the southern part of the Valley is called the "upper Valley," the northern part the "lower".) However, a region of similar landscape and way of life extends well beyond this watershed—south through Lexington to Roanoke, west across the mountains of Highland and Bath Counties, east along the upper reaches of the James River, and north into the West Virginia counties of Berkeley and Jefferson. The portrait in this book encompasses the broader area as well as the Valley strictly defined.

The Valley has other dimensions that shape its special magic. One is the dimension of time and telling, a highway into the past dwindling first to a dirt road and then to a footpath ending in the forests of myth. The name itself partakes of the mythical: some claim the word *shenandoah* harks back to a Native American legend and means "daughter of the stars," as we have subtitled this volume; but its origin is really quite unknown.

Fact and legend mingle easily in the history of the Valley: in the lore of the settlers and their tragic encounter with those who were here before them; in tales of Civil War heroics, the blue and the gray in titanic struggle up and down the Valley; in the saga of the mountain folks wrenched from the Blue Ridge; more recently, in the musical and the movie *Shenandoah;* all of this in harmony with the haunting sea chantey of the same name. The figures that personify this history also have an aura of the legendary: the Native Americans, Daniel Boone the frontiersman, George Washington the young surveyor, Stonewall Jackson the Confederate general, Cyrus McCormick the inventor, Woodrow Wilson the president. At the same time, history is a physical presence in the Valley, concrete and visible, embodied in the works of countless little-known or unknown men and women over the centuries, from the ceremonial mounds of the Native Americans to the stone houses of the Quakers and Mennonites to the spectacular road carved out along the crests of the Blue Ridge.

And then there is the dimension of the Valley's natural beauty, unforgettable to anyone who has visited there: soft blue mountains east and west; rolling green hills and fields; splashes of wildflowers blowing easily in the breeze; the shallow lazy river meandering, seemingly as it wishes; the lush foliage of the forests with warm pink traces of mountain laurel; the delicate ferns and orchids. This is nature at its most benign, a comfortable land, a land that fits human perspective. The size and scope of the Valley simply seem right—the abundant water, the open fields, the inviting forests, the mild seasons. If we have not always treated the Valley as kindly as it treats us—and I have cringed at the lack of consideration some show the land—it is nevertheless a place where, more than in most places, the natural order and human beings are in harmony.

In my photography I used no filters and no artificial light with my Leica cameras. There were no darkroom manipulations. I did sometimes employ long lenses. My goal was simply to show the Valley as it is, in representative images.

Julia Davis Adams' poetic book *The Shenandoah,* so beautifully written half a century ago, is a treasure to me and, as abridged by the author, forms the text of this volume. Our interpretations of the Valley meshed wonderfully, even though we arrived at them quite independently. Her careful abridgment, a task remarkable in itself so late in her life, was a labor of love for the Valley. Shortly after completing it, Mrs. Adams went dancing and suffered a stroke that proved fatal. She was ninety-two years old. We all are richer for her existence and her writing. Thank you, Julia . . .

I wish to thank Frank and Audrey Buckles, who have been an inspiration to me for over twenty-five years. I also thank biologists Tom Blount of the National Park Service and Robert Glasgow, Ron Hughs, and Gary Norman of the National Forest Service. The staffs of Luray and Skyline Caverns were very helpful, as were the historical societies of Winchester, Rockingham, Jefferson, and Warren Counties. My gratitude to Ben Ritter and Warren Hofstra for reviewing the accuracy of the text. Nancy Melton of the Winchester Tourism Office was a wonderful source. Mike Vaughan, Mike Schrage, and

Amy Deller of Virginia Polytechnic Institute helped me with the bears. Joe Grandstaff of the Virginia Museum of Frontier Culture, in Staunton, was very kind. Sandy Izer of the National Jousting Hall of Fame helped in her unusual field. Thanks also to Catherine Fry of LSU Press for believing in this project, to Rich Hendel for the book's design, and to Gerry Anders for his sensitive editing.

My wife, Joan, who left her heart in the Valley, contributed greatly to the book's completion. So did my son, Lucian, who accompanied me on a tour and pointed out many of the things I photographed. I thank my good friend Leo Lamer, who keeps prodding me onward. And I thank the Valley: it has placed a torch in my soul, which flame will not go out while I remain on earth.

Lucian Niemeyer

Shenandoah

Oh, Shenandoah, I long to hear you,
Away, you rolling river!
Oh, Shenandoah, I'm going to leave you,
Away, I'm bound away,
'Cross the wide Missouri.
—"Shenandoah"

Song

It is a sailor's chantey, a lost and hungry chantey, a song of faraway men reminding themselves of things they have loved, a sea song to an inland river that never meets the sea. Its melody has the nostalgic music inherent in the name of Shenandoah—for the name, the song, and the river have a talismanic quality.

The Shenandoah is a short river, a narrow river, a shallow river. No commerce rides its often-muddy waters, no cities break the willow fringe along the banks. Yet to thousands who have never seen it, the Shenandoah is music, the Shenandoah is romance.

The Shenandoah is a legend, and it deserves to be. There are names that ring like bells in history, and the Shenandoah is one of them, for it is not only a river, but also a valley, a valley consecrated by the lifeblood of human beings.

During four autumns and five springs, the Federal and Confederate, blue and gray, died in the Valley for their country, for their homes, and the soil is sacred now to North and South alike. Out of their courage and their pain on this symbolic battlefield rose a united nation welded by blood and fire. In the Valley of the Shenandoah we learned that we are indivisible.

The Shenandoah is a legend, and it is history. It is all the brave men and women who have loved

The South Fork, near Luray.

and walked the Valley. The roster of great names is a long one: Spotswood, Fairfax, Washington, Jefferson, Madison, Andrew Jackson, Boone, the Lincolns, Houston, Sevier, Lee, Stonewall Jackson, Sheridan, Rumsey, Maury, McCormick, Wilson, the Byrds. In all these lives the Valley has had a place. It has been a seedbed and a school for our nation.

But the legend and the history do not account entirely for the nostalgia that haunts the name of Shenandoah. The Valley is the earth itself, fecund, rewarding, rolling in gentle checkered fields to the Blue Ridge that guards it like a wall. Blue is the color for the Valley, blue mountains in the summer haze, blue sky, and cornflowers catching the sky on their petals, blue-green orchards making a festival of spring.

In the Valley are old names, old places, an old and undemanding way of living. It is land that has been loved rather than exploited, and for that reason it has given to its residents the best that land can give: stability, and a treelike peace that has no cause to fear the slow swing of the seasons. Life moves at its own tempo in the Valley, not with the brief fevered grasping of an individual span. The Blue Ridge rocks are old, and the river has survived great changes. The earth is old to cultivation, but it is not exhausted, for it has been cherished.

More than history, the Valley is a way of life. It is the rich fields, and the mountains older than measured time. It is the stillness of a hot noon, or of moonlight, or of snow. It is the calm old houses, where the oak leaves and the doves have time to set up their music in the heart of a child.

The Valley is home.

*Meems Bottom, south of
Mount Jackson, Shenandoah
County, looking east toward
Massanutten Mountain*

The hills are shadows, and they flow
From form to form, and nothing stands;
They melt like mist, the solid lands,
Like clouds they shape themselves and go.
—Tennyson, In Memoriam

CHAPTER 2

The Unrecorded Past

The Shenandoah River flows northward for 150 miles through a valley in Virginia between the Blue Ridge and the Allegheny Mountains, and meets the Potomac at Harpers Ferry, the convergence of Virginia, West Virginia, and Maryland, 50 miles from Washington. At Harpers Ferry it brawls noisily over a rocky bed, but farther upstream in places it is green and still, with splendid reaches where the willows and sycamores dabble in the silent water and black bass leap abundantly. The Blue Ridge, covered with oak and hickory, hangs close to the eastern bank, and the rich fields stretch westward. At Front Royal the river is split into two branches by Massanutten Mountain, a huge monadnock rising steeply from the Valley floor. The North Fork, narrow, sluggish, deep, drains the lush bottomland of the main valley and loops itself into the spectacular Seven Bends near Woodstock. The South Fork, swifter and clearer, flows through the narrow Luray Valley on the eastern side of Massanutten.

The Shenandoah was no barrier to exploration and settlement, for it has always been easily crossed at many fords. Along both sides of the gently rolling farmland, the wooded hills rise steeply. At no point in the Valley can one be unconscious of these guardians, yet they are not close enough to be oppressive. At the wide northern end the distance between the ramparts is so great that only one range is visible at a time. The Shenandoah looks like a protected valley especially designed for security and peace.

Redbud, a colorful harbinger of spring along the Skyline Drive

The unexpected bulk of Massanutten, an isolated ridge forty miles long in the middle of the valley, increases the fortresslike aspect. Stonewall Jackson made use of it. Inside the northern arms of Massanutten lies a dell ten miles square, completely hidden from the outside world, Fort Valley. Legend says that George Washington dreamed of it as his ultimate retreat when the Revolution was going badly.

Green, fair, and sweetly varied with field and meadow, mountain and living stream, the Shenandoah Valley has seemed a good land to all who have seen it—small enough to be loved foot by foot with an intimacy denied to more sweeping landscapes, large enough to be welcoming. When Governor Spotswood of Virginia looked down from the Blue Ridge in 1716, he saw a promise in the grassy prairies edged with woodland. The early settlers found the promise to be true.

Today the mountains are still so much a wilderness that they remain a botanist's paradise, but in the Valley the buffalo grass has been crowded out by the bluegrass the English settlers brought. The dense forests have been reduced to groves of noble oaks. The story of the Valley, from wilderness to frontier, to prosperity, to disaster, to prosperity again, has been a microcosm of American history. Most of our national problems have been reflected in its life.

It took a long time to make this simple, smiling valley—perhaps a half billion years of timeless process. Some of the earliest shellfish left their fossils in the Cambrian dolomite on the valley floor. Some of the first plants left the imprints of their fernlike leaves in the much later Carboniferous shale. The Blue Ridge Mountains are made of primitive volcanic rock as old as any in existence.

In the time that geologists call "Archeozoic" because it predates all else on earth, a land mass stretched eastward over space now covered by the Atlantic Ocean. Beneath it were the granite and the gneiss, once molten, that had crystallized as the planet cooled. And there was no life anywhere.

For thousands of centuries the earth spun. Gradually a portion of this land sank below sea level, and the waters from the southern Gulf and the Atlantic seeped in to cover it from New York to Alabama

*Passage Creek in Fort
Valley, a small valley lying in
the Massanutten Mountains*

*Raven's Roost, near milepost
11 on the Blue Ridge Parkway*

*Crabtree Falls, Blue Ridge
Parkway near milepost 30*

*Whitetail doe at Mathews
Arm, Shenandoah National
Park*

with a huge landlocked sea, the Alleghenies of today below its waves. The land to the east separated the Atlantic from this Paleozoic sea. Then the rains fell, the winds blew, rivers ran, and the highlands slowly washed away. All this took time, perhaps more than three hundred million years. When the sea received the detritus from quartz mountains, sandstone was formed. When the clear and quiet waters filled with life, millions of tiny shells decomposed and hardened into limestone. Silently and imperceptibly the strata of the east coast of America formed, until six thousand feet had been laid down, and a new era dawned. The movement of the continent of Africa pushed the rocks westward, folded them upon one another as if they were dough. The waters rolled away from the upheaving land. A new range of mountains lifted and began again to wash away. These were the "mother Appalachians," of which now only the roots remain.

The granite Blue Ridge resisted erosion, so that today they display what geologists call "the convex softened contours of mature mountains." On Stony Man, the highest Blue Ridge peak, now four thousand feet above sea level, are traces of the oldest plain created by erosion after the "Appalachian revolution." The Alleghenies are made by a huge fold of sandstone harder than the surrounding shale and limestone, and the same hard sandstone forms Massanutten, which once was part of the same range.

The streams of this region originally drained it to the east and south, but the Shenandoah, then a sporadic young torrent, began at Harpers Ferry with a gully that turned itself into a gulch, cut its channels up the Valley, and "pirated" the heads of the earlier rivers by undercutting and diverting their waters into its own. From this process came the numerous "wind gaps" in the Blue Ridge—openings

Wild columbine, Skyline Drive

The area known as The Oaks, near milepost 59 on the 107-mile Skyline Drive

American bison, Harrisonburg. The Valley was once an important hunting ground for many Native American tribes, plentiful in buffalo and wapiti (elk), but few of these large animals remained by the time the European settlers arrived.

The Shenandoah Valley in spring, seen from the Skyline Drive near Browntown, Warren County. Because the river flows north, the southern part of the Valley is called the "upper Valley," the northern part the "lower Valley."

Sherando Lake Recreation Area of the George Washington National Forest, along the Blue Ridge Mountains near Waynesboro in Augusta County. The recreation area offers excellent fishing and camping.

now high and dry above the floor that were once the channels of vanished rivers. Finally the Shenandoah flowed north where it joined the Potomac as it made its way around the new mountain chain.

Water has ceaselessly sculpted more than the surface of the Valley. Under the ground, uncounted rivers once ran through the limestone, dissolving the rock with the sulphuric acid in their waters, hollowing out caverns. The Natural Bridge is part of one such cave, with the roof fallen in.

The mountains stood still and the seas subsided. The rivers cut their curving channels through the hills. Thousands of years passed like one night of impenetrable obscurity, and then there were people in the valley. No one knows how they came there, nor from what cradle of the human race they sprang. They had a more highly organized society than the tribes that followed them. They built cities that enclosed fifty acres behind earthen walls, they used copper and silver, pipes carved in shapes of tropical animals, ceremonial mounds symbolically sculpted. Then they were gone, and the chance acorns that fell on their mounds grew into trees that marked six centuries before the first European arrived. The Delawares and the Catawbas, the Algonquins and the Iroquois did not remember them.

Mountain laurel, Skyline Drive

It was not in the Shenandoah Valley that these early builders raised their pyramids, their ceremonial circles, their human figures seventy feet long. But they lived in the Valley and left burial mounds behind them. In the early 1800s a citizen of Winchester named William Pidgeon made himself into an amateur archaeologist. He opened a mound nine miles from his home and found a stone vault in the center, full of bones. The railroad destroyed it when they built on their right of way, but four miles west of Winchester, under another mound of stone, workers found a limestone basin eight feet in diameter and deeply marked by fire. On the North Fork stood still another mound, and on the South Fork a moat and a wall, remnants of a ceremonial circle. The earliest historians of the Valley mention these remains as having been "reduced by the plow." The seated skeletons, the earthen vessels, the pipes with twining serpents were looked at curiously, and lost.

When Europeans came, they found the Valley almost empty, used as a hunting ground and a roadway between northeast and southwest. There was a well-marked trail along the top of the Blue Ridge, where the Skyline Drive now runs, and another trail in the valley, now the Valley Pike. The Shawnees

Buffalo Creek, Route 251 near Murat, Rockbridge County

Dogwood in bloom, Highland County

Redbuds and spring foliage in the Blue Ridge

Countless mountain streams provide the flow that creates the Shenandoah River.

Autumn storm building along the Skyline Drive

maintained three villages near Winchester, three collections of bark huts near little clearings where straggling corn and pumpkins grew. Another Shawnee village stood near Woodstock, and the Tuscaroras occupied the neighborhood of Martinsburg.

The white newcomers heard legends of a people called the Senedos, who had been exterminated by the Iroquois, and occasionally a trader found a tribal slave who claimed to have been a Senedo. The Cherokees had a tradition of having lived there until the northern Indians drove them farther south. There were also stories of a struggle between the Powhatans from the Eastern Shore and the Iroquois.

The Monocans called the Natural Bridge "the Bridge of God," for according to their tradition it had been thrown across the chasm for them when they were fleeing from the Powhatans.

Naked Creek Falls, near Jollett, Page County

All this the European settlers got by hearsay. The Indians they knew in the Valley were the Delawares from the Susquehanna and the Catawbas from South Carolina, who passed to and fro hunting and sometimes fighting, according to immemorial custom. Indians came and went, demanding bread and milk at the cabins where they stopped, regarded as nuisances, regarded as jokes, boasting about their exploits. They claimed to have fought a great battle at Painted Rock near Harpers Ferry, where their blood had reddened the stones forever. The Catawbas said they had buried a Delaware chief alive near Shepherdstown, where a spring flowed from the pulsing of his heart. At Parrill's farm, near Winchester, thirty Delawares passed through with a Catawba prisoner. Soon the Catawbas were on their trail, followed them up the mountain, killed them, and stopped at Parrill's with their rescued comrade on the way south again. At another farm, the Delawares came through with a Catawba woman tied with grapevines, on the ends of which they slept at night to keep her from escaping. Near a settlement they sacrificed her and her child. They cut off the soles of the dead woman's feet so that she could not follow them over the mountains.

Ignorant heathen, scarcely more human than wolves, the whites thought them. Thomas Jefferson deduced that war must be the natural state of humankind, since these "savages" fought even though they dwelt six hundred miles apart and had "no trade, commerce or clashing of interests." To the eyes of the pioneer, the Valley was empty. It must be made into a dwelling place for man—and "man" did not mean a handful of naked savages.

The Indians left little in the Valley—mounds to be plowed under, arrowheads, the dust of bones. Only one imperishable trace of them remains. They left the Valley its name, Shenandoah.

The name has evolved, like most American place names of Native American origin. Old records give many phonetic spellings: Gerando, Gerundo, Shendo, Genantua, Sherando. Many meanings have been assigned to it. The most romantic one, the one popularly accepted by the Valley people themselves, is "Daughter of the Stars." As Daughter of the Stars the river has been enshrined in the hearts of Valley dwellers, and as Daughter of the Stars, it will remain to them.

*From this discourse it is clear that the long looked for discovery of the Indian Sea doth
nearly approach.*
—John Lederer to William Talbot, 1670

CHAPTER 3

Exploration

&uropeans had been sixty years established on the lowlands of the coast. Their foot-
hold on the continent was secure.

In 1669 a German named John Lederer, born in Hamburg, came to Sir William Berkeley, then
governor of Virginia, and procured a license to trade furs across the mountain wall at the west of the colony. At that time everyone knew that North America was divided into three parts—"the flats, the
highlands, and the mountains, called by the Spaniards Apalatean." All reasonable people considered
the mountains impassable, but when the March sun began to bring out a mist of young leaves, Lederer
left York River with three Indian guides and vanished in the tangled green thickets.

The party made its way across the highlands. By March 14 they reached the mountain crest and
peered down out of the woods into a shining valley, green with young grass, and far across it in the hazy
distance, climbing waves of purple mountain peaks. The guides prostrated themselves on the ground
crying, "God is nigh." After going three days farther, enough to discover that the mountains were
apparently endless, Lederer returned to tell the governor what he had seen.

On May 20 he started out again, this time with a larger party: a Major Harris, "twenty Christian
horses," and five guides. They came again over the mountains and descended to a river, which Harris

Skunks are bold foragers for food in the Shenandoah National Park.

Whitetail fawns are a relatively common sight along the Skyline Drive, delighting tourists.

The South Fork meandering through one of its many bends, near Grove Hill, Page County

identified as "an arm of the lake of Canada." When he had seen this much, he was ready to go back. Lederer persisted in following the river to the south. Major Harris stuck it out for two more days, then led his party homeward, leaving his German friend to advance on foot with a lone guide. Harris wrote Lederer down as a lost man.

For two months Lederer made his way southward, living happily among the Indians. He discovered that they had been driven down from the northwest by their enemies and, as they liked to tell it, had been led to this green land by an oracle. They measured time with knotted cords, and used hieroglyphics: a stag for swiftness, a serpent for wrath, a dog for fidelity, a swan for the English, who had flown over the sea.

They were kind to Lederer, and he treated them with respect. When he saw strange things, he kept silent. He saw an ambassador and five other men of the Rickohockans arrive to treat with the Akenatzy. He saw the withy council lodge darkened by the smoke of a great feast, under cover of which all the strangers were murdered. Lederer saw this and departed quietly with his guide that night, not troubling to say farewell. Later, the Tuscaroras took his gun, but this did not alarm him, as he reasoned that one gun had no real value against so many potential enemies. He journeyed on until he was told that the Spaniards lived to the southwest, only two days away. He was not afraid of the Indians, but he did fear the Spaniards, so he turned back and came out near Appomattox, "not a little overjoyed to see Christian faces again."

Apple blossoms, Clarke County

John Lederer had not had enough. Since he had found a pass through the southern "Apalateans," he thought that there must be one to the north.

In August of 1670 he set out a third time, now with a Colonel Catlett, "nine Christian horses, five Indians." They crossed the Blue Ridge easily at Manassas Gap and descended into broad savannas and flowery meadows. The grass that sprang from the limestone soil was so high they could tie it across their saddles. Since the Indians burned this land every autumn to make their game preserve, it was only lightly wooded with occasional groves of oak or maple. Lederer was bitten by a spider, and although one of the Indians saved him by sucking the wound, after an illness he was persuaded to turn back.

This time he did not meet a pleasant welcome in Virginia. Major Harris had been explaining why he had given up when another man found it possible to continue alone, and Lederer was written down as a "presumptuous stranger." From a storm of "affronts and reproaches" he fled to Maryland, where Lord Calvert received him hospitably. Virginia and Maryland were then, as ever in colonial days, jealous of each other and engaged in boundary disputes.

Time passed into another century, and still the mountains remained a barrier to be crossed only by occasional traders—quiet men who did not talk or write about their journeys.

In 1707, French Louis Michelle and a party from Annapolis came through the gap at Harpers Ferry and traveled south as far as Fort Valley. A crude map from the journey made its way to the Public Record Office in London. Michelle's group heard a name, "Senantoa," applied to the mountains, they found evidence of silver mines, but they recorded nothing more. By 1716 they had been forgotten. Time was ripe for another expedition. This was to be discovery in a different style, with dash and a flourish rare in American annals, headed by His Honor the Governor of Virginia.

Even the background of Governor Alexander Spotswood had a romantic richness. He was descended from a Scottish archbishop who had been deposed, but later buried in Westminster Abbey. He was born

Passage Creek, Fort Valley, in its fall colors

in Tangier, wounded at Blenheim, fought at Malplaquet, rose to be quartermaster general for Marlborough at the age of twenty-eight. When he came to Virginia in 1710, he was ambitious for the improvement of the colony. In 1716 he boldly determined to attempt the passage of "the great mountains" to establish Virginia's western claims. This would be official discovery, stamped with the royal seal.

Late in August, at Germanna on the Rapidan, His Honor assembled his party, fifty strong: gentlemen, servants, Indian guides, two companies of rangers, horses, and "abundant provisions." Spotswood wore a riding habit of green velvet, boots of Russian leather, and a hat with a fine plume. The names of the gentlemen who rode with him read like a Virginia roster of today: Beverly, Robertson, Robinson, Taylor, Todd, Mason, Brooke, and young Ensign John Fontaine, who did posterity the kindness of keeping a diary.

First Fontaine listed the "abundant provisions": several cases of Virginia wine, both white and red, Irish *usquebaugh*, brandy, stout, two kinds of rum, champagne, cherry punch, cider, etc. Then he recounted how the group had had the foresight to shoe their horses with iron, for the mountain trails would be rough. At seven on the morning of August 30, the expedition sprang to life at the call of a trumpet. "We had lain on the ground under the cover of our tents, and we found by the pains in our bones that we had not had good beds to lie on." By nine they had sent the servants and the baggage forward, but the gentlemen remained behind to catch the governor's horses, which had strayed. By two-thirty they had secured the horses, by three they mounted, by half past four they came up with the baggage at a small river. Exhausted by an arduous day of one and one-half hours of travel, they found at the river "good pasturage for our horses, and venison in abundance for ourselves." The next day, inured to woodland life, they covered fourteen miles, and so continued until by September 2 they found themselves actually toiling up the mountains. Alas now for the riding habits of green velvet, the plumes, the boots of Russian leather—the thickets tore clothing, and even saddles and holsters, to shreds: "We had a rugged way."

They were not men to turn back, and by September 6, they looked out above the leaves at Swift Run Gap, higher than a buzzard that soared by on silent outstretched wings. In the surrounding woods, the Virginia creeper, already touched by frosty nights, flung scarlet cascades down the trees, but the smiling unknown valley lay still in midsummer.

His Honor observed the occasion properly. He called a halt, drank to the health of the king, drank to the health of the royal family, then led his party down the slopes between the crouching hills. They found the descent harder than they had expected, for the little streams led to precipices too steep for the horses, but at length they reached the valley floor, pushed through the waving grass, and camped by a clear and beautiful river, which they named "Euphrates." Fortunately, Governor Spotswood was an explorer and not a settler, and this affected cognomen did not fasten on the Shenandoah.

The party crossed the river and buried on the other side a bottle that contained a paper claiming all this territory for His Majesty King George I. They feasted on deer and wild turkey and on the cucumbers, currants, and grapes that grew around them. "We had a good dinner, and after it we got the men together and loaded all the arms; and we drank the King's health in champagne, and fired a volley; and the Princess in burgundy, and fired a volley; and all the rest of the Royal Family in claret, and fired a volley. We drank the Governors health, and fired another volley."

Sugar maple, Highland County. Brilliant in the fall, sugar maples are tapped for their sap in the spring.

Skyline Drive, fall. Many tourists time their visits to coincide with the fall foliage season.

In the pleasure of retrospect, Governor Spotswood wrote glowingly about his trip to what he called "World's End": "The chief aim of my expedition . . . was to satisfy myself whether it was practicable to come at the Lakes. . . . I discovered by the relations of Indians who frequent those parts . . . that from the western side of one of the small mountains which I saw the Lake is very visible."

Encouraged by this bit of misinformation, His Honor hoped that they might soon establish an English trading post that would drive a wedge between the extremities of the French position. He ordered little golden horseshoes for the gentlemen who had gone with him, and inscribed them "Sic Juvat Transcendere Montes," in memory of their preparation for the "rugged way." And so with waving plumes and convivial volleys, the governor and his "Knights of the Golden Horseshoe" ride out of the story.

Settlement

There were three great strains in the early settlement of the Shenandoah Valley: two were the Germans and the Scotch-Irish, both Protestant with long traditions of religious persecution and a hatred of European quarrels; the third group were English settlers of gentle blood. The Germans, among whom were some Swiss, came first.

In 1689 the Catholic soldiers of Louis XIV drove the Protestants from the Palatinate. Some fled to England and then on to the New World. These German Protestants were careful people, serious people, who intended to work hard and to establish their families on a solid basis. Between 1726 and 1735, many of them entered the valley of the "Cenanto" in small groups, all searching for the same thing: land that could be improved.

They did not come into the Valley over the forbidding wall of mountains, but in a more natural way, down through the rolling fields of Pennsylvania, fording the Potomac near what is now Shepherds-town, which the Germans called Mechlenburg. An old tombstone indicates that there were settlers there as early as 1726, but their record has been lost. They knew good land when they saw it, these Germans who had so little, who brought with them only their will to work, their healthy flock of children, a domestic animal or two, a few household utensils, and their massive German Bibles with clasps of brass or iron. They pushed southward up the Valley, and their children's children remain there to this day, holding the two things left to them: the land and the heavy German Bibles.

Most of the settlers were obscure people, and their arrival is veiled in obscurity. It appears that after those at Mechlenburg came the Swiss Adam Miller, whose application for a naturalization certificate in 1731 stated that he had lived five years in the "fields of Massanutten." History records of him one other fact: the house he built for his family burnt down on the day that he was to move in, and he patiently began that night to build another.

John Van Meter, a fur trader, saw the waving grasses five feet high and obtained a grant in 1730 for 10,000 acres in the fork of the "Sherando." A year later he sold his grant to a German of some wealth

Hopewell Friends Meeting, Clearbrook, Frederick County. Quakers were among the first European settlers in the Valley, arriving in the early 1730s north of Winchester.

Meeting room,
Hopewell Friends Meeting

The White House, Route 211 near Luray. The earliest European settlers of the Valley built a fort here in the late 1720s.

and substance, Hans Jost Heydt. Joist Hite, to Anglicize him as his neighbors did, came from Alsace to Kingston, New York, in 1710. Hite moved southward little by little, crowded here, discouraged there by Indian raids, until in October of 1731, "cutting his road from York," he crossed the Potomac and settled near the Quakers, five miles southwest of the site of Winchester. Of the sixteen families who came with him, three were families of his sons-in-law, George Bowman, Paul Froman, and Jacob Chrisman. Four were the families of his sons. In partnership with a Quaker named Robert McKay and others, he increased his holdings to 100,000 acres.

Joist Hite behaved like a man who had come to stay. At first he lived in a log cabin like the other settlers, but before long he began to quarry stones for the foundation of his barn. After the stock had been taken care of, he quarried for his permanent stone house, the first built in the Valley.

The Germans in the middle of the Valley held stubbornly to their own ways. In some places they clung to their language for more than a hundred years. They slept between feather comforters, ate sauerkraut, wore short coats with long waistcoats above their breeches, trimmed their broad hats with heavy silver buckles. As with all back-country people, their weddings were their great social occasions. When one of the Miller girls married near Woodstock, they danced for a week, after the toast: "Here's health to the groom, not forgetting myself, health to the bride, thumping luck, and big children."

The Germans loved their thumping big families, worked them hard, and built for the future. They were the best of settlers, say the old records, because of their thrift and "their perfect submission to the civil authorities."

The Scotch-Irish, who for the most part settled in the upper Valley, may have admired this submissiveness, but they did not imitate it. It has been said that the Covenanters, whose descendants they were, had such a fear of God that it left no room in their hearts for any fear of man. From the persecutions of Dundee, in Scotland, they had fled to Ulster. They soon quarreled with the Catholic Irish, and they survived the siege of Londonderry. Catholic monarchs tried to exterminate them. Anglican monarchs called them dissenters, held their marriages illegal, barred them from office or military rank. If they could not live in Scotland, they would move to Ulster. If they could not live in Ireland, they would migrate to America. If they could not live in Pennsylvania, they would move to Virginia. They made not the slightest modification of their beliefs, they bowed to no temporal authority. Still Presbyterians, they moved on to the south and west.

They moved on to the almost empty Valley. By 1738, the year when the first Valley counties were established, they were in such numbers that they sent the governor of Virginia a petition: "For those who are of the same persuasion as the Church of Scotland . . . to ask your favor in allowing them the liberty of their consciences, and of worshiping God in a way agreeable to the principles of their education."

The governor graciously replied that they would not be interfered with as long as they behaved peaceably, registered their meeting place, and abjured the Stuart pretender, the doctrine of transubstantiation, and the pope in Rome. Nothing in this decree disturbed the Presbyterian conscience, and the Scotch-Irish in turn agreed to pay tithes to the Established Church—as long as they did not have to go to it.

There was no one to object to the Scotch-Irish in the Valley, and this time they found rest; not only they, but numerous other small and unpopular sects, notably the Quakers and the Mennonites. The Germans called "Dutch" and the Scotch called "Irish" were glad to have neighbors.

First among the Scotch-Irish, like Joist Hite among the Germans, was John Lewis, who founded the town of Staunton in 1732. Strictly speaking, he was not Scotch-Irish at all, for he was of French descent, and his wife, Margaret, came from Loch Lynn in Scotland; but he had lived in the north of Ireland, and he had left in a hurry, for he had killed his landlord, Lord Clonmithgairn. There had been an argument over rents, the courts upheld Lewis, the lord attacked him in Clonmell Castle at night, and in the ensuing fight Lewis lost his brother and Clonmithgairn his life. Lewis fled, and found refuge in Virginia. When he arrived, he stayed in Williamsburg with Governor Gooch, a friend of his wife's family, and there he heard about the Shenandoah from John Peter Salling, a Marco Polo of the wilderness who had been captured in the Valley by some passing Iroquois and taken as far as the Mississippi. Salling's story of the rich land induced Lewis to obtain a grant and cross the mountains with about thirty of his tenantry. They built their cabins where the flowering prairie "unrolled like gaudy carpeting around them." The brave and gentle Margaret Lewis consoled her loneliness by keeping a diary, a "Book of Comforts," between the lines of an old ledger. In it she tells how she set to work to make her home beautiful for her children, so that they might love to stay in it "and learn beauty of soul by growing up with beautiful things." When she transplanted some wild roses to bloom around the door, Oroonah, the Indian chief who lived nearby, told her that she should have left them alone, for the Great Spirit had put the flowers where he wanted them.

The Scotch-Irish were religious and contentious, but they were not too grim to enjoy a wedding. Margaret Lewis went to the nuptials of John Peter Salling's nephew, where they had whiskey in a barrel

Joist Hite home, Route 11, Frederick County. Hite led a band of settlers into the Valley in 1731. He first erected a log cabin, then in 1737 built this stone manor house, Springdale.

and a gourd for a ladle, where they danced reels and jigs while the fiddler played "Hang Out Until Morning."

Margaret's baby Charles, born in Virginia, she called her "New World child," but although she did not realize it, all her sons were New World children. This wilderness life, the harshness of which she attempted in her gentle way to modify, would claim them all. John Lewis lived long and when he died they carved on his headstone an epitaph like a trumpet call:

Restored log cabin in Winchester on land once owned by Abraham Hollingsworth. Hollingsworth's stone manor house, Abram's Delight, was built in 1754.

HERE LIES THE REMAINS OF JOHN LEWIS

WHO SLEW THE IRISH LORD

SETTLED IN AUGUSTA COUNTY

LOCATED THE TOWN OF STAUNTON

AND FURNISHED FIVE SONS TO FIGHT THE BATTLES OF

THE AMERICAN REVOLUTION

In 1736 Lewis was visited by one Benjamin Burden, an agent for Lord Fairfax. Burden was delighted with the Valley and supposedly brought back a baby buffalo as a present for Governor Gooch. The governor rewarded him with a "minor grant" of 500,000 acres on the Shenandoah and the upper James, provided that he could settle one hundred families on it within ten years. Each family would receive a hundred acres, with the privilege of taking up a hundred more as soon as five acres of the first were planted in corn and His Majesty received a rent of two shillings an acre. Since there were no surveyors to establish boundaries, successive governors granted land without regard to what had been done before, thereby laying the foundation of a conviction in American minds that royal government was something they could do without.

Burden soon brought his first shipload of settlers from northern Ireland. Like the Germans, the Scotch-Irish had come to stay.

Soon after John Lewis laid out Staunton, a group of Scotch, Welsh, and English settlers founded a town in the lower Valley. Their leader was Colonel James Wood, who had been educated at Oxford, had served in the Royal Navy, and had come to the Valley in his late twenties as a surveyor. In 1735 he began to build his "seat," Glen Burnie, beside a little brook. He eventually named it for his English home: Winchester.

Wood deeded twenty-two lots of half an acre each, crossed by two streets thirty-two feet wide, to settlers on condition that the owners should build within two years a house not smaller than twenty by sixteen feet "of framed work or square logs, dovetailed." This title, said the deed with premonitory foreboding, was to be defended against all claimants except Lord Fairfax.

Where were the Indians while this was taking place, while their Valley of the Silver Water was being given away, granted, parceled out, and settled? They were there. They came and went in their shadowy way, disturbing the face of nature as little as did the deer. At first they respected the plowed fields, but as the fields stretched farther and the wild game diminished, they grew restless. Still they were prepared to tolerate these settlers, who were not the dreaded Long Knives (Virginians, named for their swords), and something like peace between the two peoples lasted for twenty years.

Of all the settlers, only the Quakers and Mennonites made serious efforts to purchase the land from those it had nurtured so long. In 1738 leader Thomas Chaulkly wrote a letter to his brethren on the Opequon, exhorting them to keep a friendly correspondence with the Indians and pay them fairly, "for as nature hath given them and their forefathers the possession of the continent . . . they had a natural right thereto in justice and equity." Clearly this devout old man, with his talk about natural rights and honest purchase, was not in touch with reality as his contemporaries saw it. Who could make binding agreements with savages? Half the time there was no one about from whom a purchase could be made. The main body of Valley settlers had a comfortable conviction of God's guidance. Plainly the Lord God of Hosts had led them to this Canaan which they would make to flow with milk and honey—or, if necessary, with blood.

CHAPTER 5

Pioneers

*A*s the years passed, life took on a pattern in the Valley—a pattern of small cabins in the clearings, of long laborious days tuned to the slow change of the seasons, of lonely silent nights broken by wolves or whippoorwills. Try to imagine the silence of the Valley, where a man could work all day with only his work for company, hearing the wind whisper, hearing the doves, hearing the corn stretch and crackle in the heat, hearing the singing silence of the earth itself. A man had his hands and arms for company, and his children helping in the fields; and for the evening, his children and his wife. His wife and time to watch the blue deepen into purple, to see the darkness slowly cover the mountains and trees.

Day and day's labors ended with darkness, and the wilderness flowed back, lapping the cabin threshold like persistent water, turning each home into an island in the night. During these hours men did not like to leave their families, and all slept close and warm together until first light came through the chinks in the shutters, and called them to stir out again in the fresh morning.

In such a society everyone welcomed new arrivals. Weddings and buryings, harvesting, log rolling, house raising, these were occasions for a feast. A newly married couple could count on all to help them build, to set the cornerstones and lay the sleepers, to raise the log walls, and lay the puncheon floor. A

Staff members of the Museum of American Frontier Culture in Staunton demonstrate pioneer sawing techniques at the Frontier Festival, an annual September event.

Millstones, Abram's Delight. Grist and flour mills powered by the Valley's streams provided an economic base for trade with the eastern population.

long porch across the front gave saddle-storage room and shade in the summer. When they had cut a loophole to fire from, hung an oaken door, built a stone chimney, and chinked the cracks, the work was done. A home could be built in three days.

Some children died in almost every family, but those who lived grew strong. The pioneers attributed the diseases of children to worms and dosed them with the scrapings of a pewter spoon. For croup, onion or garlic juice; for fever, sweating with snakeroot or purge with walnut bark; for the itch, a salve of brimstone and hog lard; for burns, a poultice of Indian meal or slippery elm; for snakebite, anything and everything. The men developed rheumatism as their moccasins, although warm enough when stuffed with leaves, became waterlogged on wet days. All backwoodsmen learned to sleep with their feet to the fire.

It was not an easy life for soft people. But the "back" inhabitants of the Valley had no intention of remaining in this primitive state. By 1734 so many of them had settled that the burgesses of Virginia established a county called Orange, and grandly declared that its borders should extend to the Missis-

Morgan's Spring, Shepherdstown, West Virginia. Shepherdstown was long a prime point of entry for settlers migrating to the Valley. Richard Morgan owned and developed this natural spring in the 1730s.

South Fork, Grove Hill, Page County. In the spring, high waters allowed bargemen to float their "gundalows" from Port Deposit downriver to the Potomac.

sippi. This did not serve, for the back inhabitants would not cross the mountains to attend court. In 1738 the burgesses revised their gesture, set the boundaries of Orange east of the mountains, and divided the wild west, "unto the utmost limits of Virginia," into two new counties, named for the Prince and Princess of Wales, Frederick and Augusta.

In 1743 courts were set up at Frederick Town (now Winchester) for Frederick County; in 1745 at Staunton for Augusta. At Frederick Town, James Wood and his friends selected justices and elected a sheriff, charging him to build a courthouse of forty-foot logs, a hut on Sheep Hill Common for the safekeeping of persons with the smallpox, and a jail, twelve by twelve—"he not to be answerable for escapes." They also ordered a roadway cut "through the dense forest out to the grassland both to north and south."

The justices were not sparing in the lashes they ordered laid on at their whipping post—twenty-five for a girl who had borne an illegitimate child. They would have the court respected, and while it sat, "no person should presume to strain either by pacing or racing through the streets." They built a ducking stool for scolds, a pit seven feet square with a roof over it. Soon the lower Valley would have all the benefits of civilization. In Augusta they offered a bounty of 100 pounds of tobacco for a wolf head, and in one month they had to pay for 225 killed wolves.

As might have been expected, the Presbyterian settlers of Augusta had taken care of their spiritual welfare before they organized their temporal affairs. When they received the governor's permission to worship freely, they importuned the Presbytery of Donegal, in Pennsylvania, to send them a minister. In 1739 they were rewarded by being allowed to call the Reverend John Craig.

Early settler's farm, Museum of American Frontier Culture. The authentic farmstead was moved to the museum from Eagle Rock, in Botetourt County.

Tobacco barn, Museum of American Frontier Culture. Tobacco was a cash crop for many early small farmers in the Valley, just as it was on the great James River plantations to the east.

Rosa Kesterson and Martha Tillen making plum butter, Frontier Festival, Museum of American Frontier Culture

A young man more thoroughly fitted to bring a wilderness into order and its souls into the fear of God could not have been discovered. In the story of his work, which he later published, he said that he had been born in Ireland, educated in Edinburgh, and "compelled at the age of five or six to fly to God with tears and prayers in secret for pardon, peace, guidance and direction." He felt himself directly guided, for while still in Scotland he had seen his future parish in a dream, and on the ship coming over, one wave had swept him off the deck and the next threw him back upon the vessel, unharmed. He was convinced that he had been preserved for some purpose, and he did not falter in pursuit of it.

By the time they built the Staunton Courthouse, Craig had three congregations, and if he could walk five miles, carrying his rifle, to preach, they could travel ten to hear him. When they arrived he

Settler's cabin, Blue Ridge Parkway near milepost 30. Many log cabins, some dating to the early days of settlement, remain in the Valley today.

Route 250, West Augusta, Augusta County

Scotch-Irish immigrants
were heavily represented
among the settlers of the
upper Valley. To help portray
the Scotch-Irish heritage, this
house was brought from
County Tyrone, Northern
Ireland, to the Museum of
American Frontier Culture.

*Mill and spring house,
Liberty Furnace. Route 717,
Shenandoah County*

gave them something worth coming for, preaching from ten in the morning until sunset, with an hour for lunch. He first preached in the open air, but soon had his people building churches. The Old Stone Church by the Valley Pike had walls thick enough for a fortress (a circumstance that later proved useful). All the men of the congregation worked on it, with their guns beside them, and the women brought the sand for the mortar on horseback from the river.

The Scotch-Irish, who had disagreed with so many people, also disagreed among themselves. Before long a schism split the church, and the New Side referred to the pastor as a "poor blind carnal hypocritical wretch." Nevertheless, John Craig remained the shepherd and leader of the upper Valley during four and twenty years.

The settlers were in general a law-abiding people, determined to organize their new communities properly, but in the matter of land grants there arose a confusion. The settlers could not be blamed for it, and contended mightily against it; yet it also gave free rein to the quality that in successful ancestors is called mother wit. For instance, in the Luray Valley, a Swiss, Jacob Stover, took up five thousand acres in the names of his horses, cows, dogs, cats, as heads of families. Others bought from him, and in 1733 a settlement petition reached Governor Gooch from the "fields of Massanutten," in the name of Abraham Strickler and a small group of settlers, complaining that, having bought from Stover, they were now being threatened with eviction by Sir William Beverly, who claimed rightful title. Although Beverly was the great landowner of the lower Valley, the governor upheld the petitioners' right to stay. Both Stricklers and Stovers live today east of Massanutten on land their forebears named "Egypt" because of its fertility—prizing their valley and their old Bibles, printed in Zurich in 1536.

Thomas, Lord Fairfax gave the settlers more serious trouble. He was a grandson of Lord Colepeper (in later generations, Culpeper) to whom Charles II had presented, with a more than usually inclusive sweep of the royal pen, a tract known as the Northern Neck, running from the sea westward over what are now twenty-two counties.

In 1736 Lord Fairfax came to visit his cousin William Fairfax at Belvoir on the James. Before long

Beeler's Mill, near Charles Town, West Virginia

Bonnie Lewandowski and Leigh Ann Bowles knitting wool, Museum of American Frontier Culture. The wool is sheared from the museum's resident population of sheep and spun on site as well.

he realized that a great many people were living on his land without paying for it. He instructed his agents to tell them either to purchase the land or to pay rent. Those who would not pay rent or purchase must move. To his astonishment, upon asserting his legal rights he heard himself denounced as a monster by those whose only claim to the property was their cultivation of it by their own risk and sweat. The matter passed into the slow jaws of the courts. In 1746 Lord Fairfax sent a party to survey his grant. In 1747 Joist Hite finished his permanent stone house on his disputed acres, and his sons also began to build in stone. Their long dispute with Fairfax would not be settled while old Hite lived, but in the end his property would be reserved for his heirs.

By this time, the settlers of Frederick and Augusta could take pride in their progress. They had a ferry across the Shenandoah and an iron furnace at Old Bloomery. They exported hemp, furs, and whiskey. In 1747 Lawrence Washington, older half brother of George, bought 700 acres in the Valley. The next year, he bought 1,300 more.

In 1748 Lord Fairfax returned from England to assume personal supervision of his property, lived on by those whom he called his "retainers." This was a different and embittered Fairfax. Tradition says that he had been jilted by an English lady and blamed his mother and grandmother for his loss. Disappointment made him a misogynist. Within a year of his arrival he established himself on his "Manor of Leeds" at his hunting lodge, Greenway Court, a one-story log house with a long veranda. He placed a white post at the crossroads—later the town of White Post—to guide his visitors, but never allowed a woman on the premises. There he lived the remaining years of his long life, issuing decrees to his

Skittles setup, Museum of American Frontier Culture. Various forms of bowling were a favorite recreation among Valley pioneers.

"retainers" and being shocked at their spirit in disregarding his wishes. For instance, when Fairfax wanted the hamlet of Stephensburg for the county seat, along came Colonel Wood, got hold of one of the justices, brought him around over a bowl of toddy, and fixed the seat at Winchester. Lord Fairfax never spoke to the justice again.

Fairfax wished to be fair, even generous. By his own standards he was a public-spirited man, but in the wilderness he was an anachronism. The inhabitants were not his retainers and had no intention of becoming so. Surrounded by such people, it is no wonder that he seemed surprised and petulant. Nevertheless, the nights were fragrant and the days were bright. His lordship fumed and fretted, argued and sued, but he did not depart. Against his volition, like many an emigrant before and since, he had been captured by the Valley.

Washington

*I*n 1748 Lord Fairfax again sent surveyors to the northern end of his Valley property. One was his cousin George William Fairfax, the other a youth of sixteen. The youth was tall, strong, serious-minded, and as the eldest son of a widow, had a lively sense of the necessity of making his own way. He came of what Virginians call "nice people." His older half brothers, one of whom had married a Fairfax, could make good connections for him, but he intended to improve his opportunities by his own hard work. His name was George Washington.

He kept a diary with a cheerful disregard of syntax and spelling:

March 15
Worked hard till night and then retired to Pennington's. We got our suppers and was lighted into a room, and I not being so good a woodsman as the rest of my company striped myself very orderly and went into the bed as they called it when to my surprise I found it to be nothing but a little straw matted together without sheets or anything else but only one threadbare blanket with double its weight of vermin. . . . I made a promise not to sleep so from that time forward chusing rather to sleep in the open air before a fire as will appear hereafter.

March 17

Rained till about 2 o'clock and cleared when we was agreeably surprised at the sight of 30 odd Indians coming from war with only one scalp. We had some liquor with us of which we gave them part it elevating their spirits put them in the humor of daucing of whom we had a war daunce. . . . There music is a pot half full of water with a deerskin over it, and a gourd with some shot in it to rattle and a piece of a horse's tail tied to it to make it look fine. . . . They hopped and carried on in a most comical manner.

Not only the Indians diverted him. Ten days later the party passed a German settlement, where the inhabitants turned out for them, and accompanied them through the woods "showing there Antick tricks. I really think they seemed to be as ignorant a set of people as the Indians. They would never speak English but when spoken to they all speak Dutch." He concluded his surveying and went back to more civilized surroundings, thinking to be finished forever with the backwoods life—but the forest, the Indians, and the frontier inhabitants had not finished with young Mr. Washington.

Route 55 near Front Royal. Prevailing high moisture content of the air often veils the Valley's distances in haze.

Greenway Court, near White Post, Clarke County. Thomas, Lord Fairfax, having received a royal grant of five million acres—including much of the Valley—settled at Greenway Court in 1751.

It was in 1754 that the Indians left the Valley—without explanation. For more than twenty years they had come and gone peacefully among the settlers. Then they were no longer there. It was as if the woods had suddenly become empty of deer.

The Valley people wondered what it could mean. They soon found out. By blood, by fire, by terror, they went on finding out for twelve long years. It was an echo of a European war. The French instigated the attacks in their efforts to hold the Ohio against English claims, bringing their rivalry rather than their settlers to this wild green land. They found no difficulty in stirring up the Indians against the English, who had been bad neighbors, never keeping a bargain, but continually pushing westward where they had promised not to go.

The French and Indian War was not continuous. There were in the Valley no pitched battles. The victims of the conflict were not soldiers, but old men, farmers, pregnant women, babies. The Indians appeared in daylight, struck and disappeared, struck again and vanished. The French paid a bounty of three pounds for a fair English scalp.

Something had to be done. Behold then, in May of 1755, lieutenant colonel George Washington, now in command of a provincial regiment, waiting in Winchester for the renowned British general Edward Braddock. Washington had already had some experience in Winchester. He had accepted a commission in the provincial army (instead of going to sea, as he had hoped to do after his surveying venture) and in 1753 had passed through Winchester on a first military mission to investigate the building of

George Washington, as an officer of the British colonial forces, used this small house in Winchester as his headquarters in 1755 and 1756, during the French and Indian War.

forts for English traders on the Ohio. The French officers with whom he had dined told him "it was their absolute design to take the Ohio and by God they would do it."

Braddock arrived, expecting to stop the Indians once and for all, having declared that "these savages may indeed be formidable to raw American militia, but against the King's regular and disciplined troops it is impossible that they should make an impression." The expedition was a disaster. Braddock started too late, moved too slowly, and was defeated at Fort Duquesne (today's Pittsburgh), where he was killed. The remnants of his force were saved by Washington, who rallied his "American militia" and covered the retreat.

In September Governor Dinwiddie returned Washington to Winchester in charge of all frontier defenses for Virginia. A full colonel and no longer amused by the war dances of the Indians, Washington spent three grueling years learning to make bricks without straw—to deal with an indifferent government, to hold an army together without pay or equipment, to act on his own responsibility when orders were not forthcoming. All America would one day have cause to be thankful for this training.

*A*fter Braddock's defeat, many of the back inhabitants gave themselves up for lost. In Pennsylvania and Maryland the frontiers were almost deserted. But the settlers along the Shenandoah were made of sterner stuff.

The Indians came to Frederick in the spring, when the oak leaves were little bigger than a mouse's ear. Eighteen or twenty of them crossed North Mountain at Mills Gap, found Patrick Kelly plowing, and killed him; found his wife milking, and killed her also. One of the children got away to give the alarm, crouching and running through the underbrush like a scared animal. Each family that heard the news rode or ran for John Evans' fort near Martinsburg. The more improvident had laughed at Evans when he laboriously cut saplings for a stockade, but they were glad to use it now.

Every year lengthened the tragic roll. Everyone knew the stories of death and near-death. There was Colonel James Patton, who had made twenty-five Atlantic crossings, surprised by six or seven Indians as he sat at a writing table with his sword in front of him; although he fought like a demon and accounted for four of them, they killed him. There was Mr. Wolfe, whose faithful dog kept him from walking into an ambush by repeatedly standing up with its paws against his chest. There were Mrs. Sheets and Mrs. Taylor, who were attacked on their way to the fort with their husbands and children. The men were both killed at the first volley, but when the Indians grabbed at the wagon, Mrs. Sheets laid about her to such a purpose with an axe and Mrs. Taylor whipped up the horses so zealously that they brought the children safely to Woodstock.

Not until 1766 did the terror stop. The last raid struck a Mennonite preacher, John Rhodes (Hans Roth). He was shot in the doorway of his house on the South Fork of the Shenandoah and fell forward, his white hair like a flag of truce across the threshold. His wife and son were shot as they tried to lift

Kitty Saufley playing harmonica between chores at the Museum of American Frontier Culture

him and another son as he climbed a tree to see what was happening. The eldest daughter caught up the baby and escaped through the barn into a field of hemp that hid her until she could cross the river.

The Indians had a music, a deep and breathing harmony with nature and the forest, but the whites could not hear it. Their tune was different, an epic of striving, of heroic determination, that would eventually become the anthem of Manifest Destiny, and that the Indians in their turn could not hear. Lost in their mutual deafness, the two peoples found no alternative to a struggle for survival that lunged on across the continent through new scenes, new men and women, new battles, until the whites prevailed, and the Native Americans vanished as a potent entity.

Fort Loudoun

When Colonel Washington took charge at Winchester he found the countryside in confusion, and he reported on it to Governor Dinwiddie: "The supplicating tears of the women and moving petitions of the men, melt me with such deadly sorrow . . . I could offer myself a willing sacrifice to the butchering enemy, provided that would contribute to the people's ease." The practical colonel set out to make soldiers of his new and undisciplined men. He sent officers to find recruits between sixteen and fifty who could meet certain physical requirements. They must not be under five feet four inches (unless well made), must not have old sores upon their legs or be subject to fits.

After a long and frustrating winter of trying to procure food, powder, uniforms, and even shoes for his troops, Washington in March asked the governor if he should take the field or build a fort, "though I have often troubled Your Honor on this head." For an expedition he would need two thousand good marksmen. He got fifteen volunteers. Fifteen volunteers and the militia. "Whooping hallooing gentleman soldiers," he called them in disgust. Since he could not resign and could not be equipped for an offensive, he strongly urged the wisdom of enfortment.

It was April and then May. Attacks continued and nothing done. Washington addressed himself to John Robinson, speaker of the Assembly, a colonist who might be more sympathetic. Robinson took an

Belle Grove, Middletown, Frederick County. Major Isaac Hite built Belle Grove in 1794 to a design by Thomas Jefferson.

Near Morgan's Ford, Clarke County

interest, and the colonel received permission to build his fort, Fort Loudoun, at Winchester. In the midst of this heartening activity, he was delayed by a custom that predated the Republic and may well survive it: the Assembly sent an investigating committee to the frontier. Washington wanted two strong forts, one at Winchester and another at Staunton. The committee instead recommended a chain of what he called "little paultry forts very expensive to maintain."

As the young colonel entered his third year of this exasperating duty, Dinwiddie sailed home. Soon after, Washington fell ill of dysentery and went to Mount Vernon, which he had inherited on the death of his half brother. There he spent a lonely winter, except for some visits to the widow Custis. April found him back on the frontier. The Assembly had augmented the frontier troops to two thousand and placed Washington in command of them with the rank of brigadier general. The long-wished-for offensive expedition was to be undertaken at last, headed by General Forbes with a force of His Majesty's regulars.

Two months passed. At the end of June, Washington was ordered to proceed as far as Fort Cumberland, eighty miles away. With high hopes the Virginia troops arrived on July 2—and remained there doing nothing until September 15. The English officers decided that instead of using Braddock's road to the Ohio, they would build a new one. Here we begin to observe the making of a good revolutionary in General Washington, a second time disappointed in the efficiency of the king's troops, and for nearly three years driven to an extremity of impatience by the royal governor. "All is lost!" he complained bitterly. "All is lost by heavens! Our enterprise ruined, and we stop'd at the Laurel Hill this winter; not to gather Laurels, by the by."

Fort Harrison, Dayton, Rockingham County. Daniel Harrison built a fort here in 1749. The site, a museum today, sits astride the Warrior Trail, used immemorially by Native Americans traveling the Valley floor.

Women's bathhouse, Warm Springs, Bath County. Native Americans eased their aches and relaxed their muscles in these warm mineral springs, and so have countless other visitors right up to this day. Thomas Jefferson designed one of the two bathhouses.

By September 1, forty-five miles of the new road had been cut. The Assembly lost interest in an expedition that had accomplished nothing. A new governor, Fauquier, arrived in Virginia and promptly received a letter from the young provincial officer: "Honored Sir: If you are surprised to find us still encamped at this place, I shall only remark that your surprise cannot well exceed my own." This communication had no effect because Governor Fauquier knew of negotiations going forward with the Indians and French that made delays advisable. Under orders, Washington proceeded to the advance post Loyal Hanna, finding the new road incredibly bad. At Loyal Hanna he learned that he and his men had been selected to open the new road through the winter woods as far as Fort Duquesne. When he was within one day's march of this objective, the enemy set the fort on fire and "ran away by the light of it down the Ohio."

By December 9, Washington had his troops back in Winchester. In his absence he had been elected to the General Assembly in Williamsburg. He resigned, not without a last plea for his men, and his officers gave him a banquet. For a second time he said farewell to the backwoods. Again he had finished, and now more firmly than ever, with military life: with the hard bed on the cold ground, rough food or none, delayed campaigns, uncertainty, discouraged men, lax subordinates, blundering civilian governments. He would take his seat in the Assembly, marry the Widow Custis, and above all, plant his fields.

CHAPTER 8

Revolution

Fort Loudoun stood on its hill, completed in spite of governors and committees. Its eighteen cannons made it so formidable that it was never attacked. In 1763 the treaty of Aix-la-Chapelle brought peace between the French and English in the New World as well as the Old. In 1764 Colonel Bouquet negotiated with the Shawnees for the release of ninety Virginia prisoners. Quiet returned to the Shenandoah for a decade, and a new type of settler began to cross the Blue Ridge.

The newcomers were gentlemen, intending to seat themselves properly on the sort of estate no longer available in the settled eastern lowlands. They had taste: they built sound, comfortable houses of brick or stone with lovely doors and mantels, and wainscoting from England. The northern end of the Valley attracted them, where the good land spread for thirty miles between the mountain ranges. The "nice people" brought their good horses and their English silver. They also brought a small, unnoticed portent of disaster: they brought slaves. (Even at that, slavery was never to be very widespread along the Shenandoah. The thrifty Germans found it wasteful; the Scotch-Irish used but few slaves.)

George Washington was responsible for some of the gentleman newcomers. Washington had great faith in the Shenandoah, representing Frederick County for two terms in the Assembly, and on his advice three of his younger brothers came to settle: John Augustine, closest in age to himself; Samuel, who married five wives, left numerous progeny, and built Harewood, where James and Dolley Madison were married; and Charles, who laid out Charles Town, named for himself.

Along the lower reaches of the Shenandoah, a marked civility of living now made its appearance, but all was not graciousness and ease. Battletown (now Berryville) became notorious for its brawls on Saturday night. Front Royal was called "Hell Town." The South Irish and the Germans rioted in Winchester. In 1771 smallpox broke out; the justices of Winchester forbade Mynn Thurston and Samuel Washington to have their families inoculated, and revoked the licenses of Drs. John McDonald and Humphrey Wells for attempting the hazardous practice.

In 1774 there was more Indian trouble on the Ohio, and the Shenandoah was still involved. The then-governor, the earl of Dunmore, organized a punitive expedition, beginning the brief episode known as Dunmore's War. After a bloody victory, the soldiers from the Valley were enraged to find that Dunmore, leading his own detachment, had made a treaty with the enemy without consulting them—and without coming to their aid.

All through the New World, men were beginning to feel that the mother country did not have their welfare at heart. When the authorities closed the port of Boston because tea had been dumped overboard, the people of Augusta County sent 137 barrels of flour by wagon to the hungry New Englanders. As early as June, 1774, a committee at Winchester solemnly protested against the official actions in Boston: "such acts would have a necessary tendency to raise a civil war, thereby dissolving that union which has so long happily existed between the Mother country and her colonies."

When the news of revolution at last reached the people of the Shenandoah, they knew what to do about it. Although disillusioned and unruly, they fought gallantly on every front and produced six generals for the cause. Less than a month after the battle of Bunker Hill, the first troops raised in Virginia left the Valley to join Washington at Boston. Captain Daniel Morgan organized one hundred sharpshooters, led them out, and by a remarkable series of forced marches, arrived there on August 7, 1775. Washington came out to review them. From Morgan down, the majority of the Virginia Riflemen had served with him in other campaigns, under Braddock, under Forbes. They were a long way from the Shenandoah now, but they were still fighting together. Tradition says that Washington shook hands with each of them in silence, and when he tried to speak, tears ran down his cheeks.

The story of Daniel Morgan is in the best American tradition. His parents were Welsh ironmongers who emigrated first to New Jersey and then to the Shenandoah. Danny Morgan had practice in rough-and-tumble. Living in Battletown after the Braddock campaign, he used to stash a pile of stones by the roadside on the way to the tavern of a Saturday night as ammunition to cover his retreat later. As the years went on he built a house called "Soldier's Rest," married, begot two daughters, and began to achieve respectability. By 1773 he owned land and slaves; in 1776 he was overseer of roads for Frederick County. Prosperity did not make him afraid of risk, as his prompt arrival in Boston demonstrated.

Morgan's Riflemen were to have a glorious history. They went through the snow with Arnold to Quebec, where Morgan and many others were captured. In time he was exchanged, and when he disembarked in New York, tradition says he knelt to kiss the soil of his country. Promoted to colonel, he led his command to Saratoga under General Gates (a neighbor from the Valley), and his sharpshooters earned a large share of credit for the victory. They were the boys who never missed with their long, muzzle-loading rifles, the boys who shot squirrels only in the right eye.

As soon as Burgoyne surrendered, the Riflemen started a forced march down the Hudson to join Washington but arrived too late for Germantown. When fighting was suspended for the winter, Morgan, who had served three years without a furlough, went home in charge of several hundred Hessian prisoners to be quartered in Winchester.

By 1780 the Revolution had dragged on for five years with no sign of ending. Some said the commander in chief did not have sense enough to give in. General Morgan took his Riflemen to fight with Gates in South Carolina. After Gates was defeated at Camden, Morgan went on to fight Tarleton at Cowpens in January, 1781. "Morgan has never been licked," he told his men. His command consisted of the Riflemen, some cavalry, and the militia. General Washington had not revised his opinion of the militia, although now he expressed it in more dignified terms. Dan Morgan knew what they were like and allowed for it. They had run on Gates at Camden and ruined him, but they were not going to ruin Danny Morgan.

Burwell-Morgan Mill, Millwood, Clarke County. Sally Trumbower, president of the Clarke County Historical Association, greets visitors to the grist and flour mill, established in 1785 and once operated by Daniel Morgan.

Potter-Wade Mill,
Effinger, Rockbridge County

He retreated until a river backed him. Then he stationed the militia three hundred yards ahead of his picked troops, ordered them to fire twice and run like the devil. Tarleton's dragoons came charging down as usual. The militia fired twice, did their running with real enthusiasm, and the dragoons over-extended themselves in pursuit just as Morgan had expected. When they were well scattered, his Rifle-men and the cavalry charged and soon had the British regulars begging for mercy. Morgan lost only twelve men.

Up in Augusta County the citizens made ready to defend themselves if Tarleton should cross the Blue Ridge. The old men and boys took up arms and went to the mountains. The sons of John and Margaret Lewis were already fighting, and now the grandsons went, down to the ten-year-old. Tarleton did not invade Augusta, and the General Assembly found refuge in the Old Stone Church. Augusta's most distinguished contribution to the Revolution had been made in the first year of the war when Brigadier Andrew Lewis and Dunmore met in battle at Gwynn's Island. This time it was not the colonial who had to retreat before he was ready.

In the Valley a new county had recently been carved from Frederick and christened Dunmore. It was quickly renamed Shenandoah. The new county produced its own revolutionary hero. In the village of Woodstock, in the middle of the Valley, lived the Reverend Peter Muhlenberg. Pennsylvania born, German educated, ordained in the Established Church, and pastor of the Lutheran flock, he interested himself in the Revolutionary movement and took part in the Virginia Convention of 1775. One Sunday after his return to the Valley, he mounted the pulpit dressed in his usual somber black robe and preached a stirring sermon on the text: "For everything there is a season . . . a time for peace, and a time for war." At the most dramatic moment, he threw off his robe, revealed himself in the uniform of a Virginia colonel, and proceeded to recruit the nucleus of a regiment from his congregation.

At the northern end of the Valley lived three men whose prospects at the beginning seemed bright, but who ultimately failed. Horatio Gates at Traveler's Rest, Charles Lee at Prato Rio, and Adam Stephen, who laid out Martinsburg, all had homes within a few miles of each other, were far above the usual rank of frontier settler, and rose to be major generals—and all three were disgraced and retired before the war ended.

Gates had come to the Shenandoah as a major in the regulars under Braddock and liked the country enough to settle there after the campaign. He persuaded his colleague Charles Lee to follow him into the neighborhood. Although Gates's parents had been only servants in the household of the duke of Leeds, he had one foot in the great world, for Horace Walpole was his godfather—some said his father. He began the war as Washington's adjutant general and displayed a talent for organization; but both he and Charles Lee considered themselves superior to their commander in chief, and in the end their careers foundered on that premise. They could not forget that they had been regulars when George was only a provincial officer.

As early as 1776, General Gates found time to inform Congress of Washington's strategic miscal-culations. While Washington struggled through the winter at Valley Forge, Gates headed a faction com-plaining that the country was being ruined "by a weak General and bad counsellors." Washington nev-ertheless put Gates in charge of driving the British from the Carolinas. Gates got himself soundly beaten by Cornwallis. Congress relieved him of command, and he retired in dignified silence to his Valley plantation; the Virginia Assembly sent him a consoling resolution.

The rise of tall, gaunt, sardonic General Lee was swifter, and his fall more steep. The son of a general in the British army, brilliant, well educated, and acutely conscious of it, he was too bright to consider himself bound by the ordinary laws of politeness, too bright to miss the mistakes of his superiors, and much too bright to conceal his observations. His military experience covered many fields, and he supported the Revolutionary cause. At the onset of war he was second in command to Washington. His successful defense of Charleston made him a hero to the public, although his ingrained belief in British superiority had almost induced him to order his soldiers to spike their guns and retire after the first volley.

During 1776, when defeat followed defeat, when the patriot army seemed to be melting away, Charles Lee retreated too slowly across New Jersey and let himself be captured by the very company of dragoons he had commanded in Spain fifteen years before. While a prisoner in New York, he was well treated, and the ever-forgiving Washington procured his exchange in the spring of 1778.

During his imprisonment, Lee had urged Congress to send him a committee "to confer on a subject of importance to the country." He told Britain's General Howe that he hoped to work out a compromise; he told the Americans that he meant to disclose to them the British plan of campaign; and he drew a map for the British showing them how take Alexandria and the Chesapeake Bay. What he meant by all this only Charles Lee knew.

When Washington fell back to Princeton, he ordered Lee to delay the enemy, but at Monmouth Court House, Lee was so impressed by reports of British strength that he retreated instead. He was falling back in some disorder when he encountered Washington and the main body of the army. That was the day when Washington swore. "He swore on that day until the leaves shook on the trees, charmingly, delightfully," one of his generals remembered. "On that memorable day he swore like an angel from heaven." On the wings of his wrath, Washington rode up and down the lines forming his men for battle—and the supposedly irresistible enemy withdrew. The day was saved, but Lee had a public dressing down. He could not let it rest. He demanded a court-martial so loudly that Washington let him have it, with the result that he was suspended for a year. The findings were sent to Congress for confirmation, and Lee talked so much that the lawmakers retired him to the life of a gentleman farmer.

Adam Stephen, who had been "nothing in the military way," did not rise so far as his two neighbors, and consequently his descent was more cushioned. He had a degree in medicine from Edinburgh. He had lived twenty years in the country, had served under Braddock, and had run successfully for the Assembly against Washington. He was astonished to find himself a major general and perhaps not too astonished when, in a fog near Germantown, his troops collided with those of Mad Anthony Wayne and he was dismissed for the error, which some were ungenerous enough to attribute to John Barleycorn.

Charles Lee once proposed a toast to the three of them: "To the one who was drunk when he should have been sober, to the one who advanced when he should have retreated, and to the one who retreated when he should have advanced."

General Gates bore his downfall in silence and was rewarded by reinstatement in 1782, in time to be at Newburgh. After the war he lived quietly in the Shenandoah for ten years, then moved to New York. Charles Lee never forgave and never accepted his fate. When Washington tried to call on him after the Revolution, he closed his shutters, locked his door and put up a sign: "No bread or bacon baked here today." Adam Stephen went on to serve in the Virginia convention that ratified the Constitution.

With three successful generals and three failures, the record does no more than balance—except that the glory of the Shenandoah during the Revolution was not in its general officers, but in its men.

Tories were rare in the Valley. The few who existed were haled into court and tried, although most were then released under bond and mildly treated. The most prominent of them, Lord Fairfax, withdrew from the county court in Frederick but lived unmolested at Greenway Court. The Quakers, Mennonites, and Dunkards opposed violence as usual, taking their customary stand against bearing arms. Yet even they could not always hold out against the patriotism and warlike temper of the Valley neighbors. Some followed wealthy Isaac Zane of Frederick, who declared himself "a Quaker for the times," served as an officer of militia, and in his iron furnace at Marlboro turned out both cannon and cannon balls.

There were, of course, slackers, as there are in every war and every era, but the Shenandoah had been settled by men fully prepared to fight for their independence. No one was drafted in the Valley under the law of 1778, for the quota had been filled by volunteers. They were valiant soldiers and wonderful shots, but not in love with discipline. George Washington had to remind General Morgan that the Riflemen must be subject to regulations like the rest of the army.

In the dramatization of our national legend, it should not be forgotten that eight years elapsed between the first shots at Lexington and the final treaty of peace at Yorktown; and at no time during that period, in spite of individual successes, did the general situation look bright for the colonists.

Every effort was made to divide the colonies by offers of peace, or to separate by diplomatic means the Americans and the French. All failed. In the end it was the British who fell apart by differences among themselves.

The Americans looked weak and they were; looked disorderly, uncouth, untutored, and they were all of these things; but they were sustained by a potent dream. They had imagined a strong and indivisible country where every citizen could walk in freedom.

In the Shenandoah Valley a leading exponent of the old order heard the news from Yorktown and knew what it meant. "Help me to bed," said the octogenarian Lord Fairfax to his servant. "It is time for me to die."

CHAPTER 9

Expansion

When the Revolution ended and the soldiers of the Shenandoah came home, they found their Valley in terrible shape. Taxes were high, markets reduced, Maryland astride the Potomac, and interstate duties made trade impossible. Everyone was in debt.

But the Valley was not ruined. The crops continued to push up through the generous soil, the doves sang in the oaks, the fructifying sun evoked abundance. The Valley began to come back.

No one expected that recovery would take place all at once. Trade expanded gradually. The legislature voted Washington a hundred shares in the James River Canal. In accord with his policy "to shut my hand against every pecuniary recompense," he promptly gave the shares to the Rockbridge academy, Liberty Hall, and the school changed its name to Washington College.

In 1786 the Court of Appeals handed down a final decision in the fifty-year-old case of *Hite* v. *Fairfax*. Fairfax was dead, Hite was dead, but the land was secured to Hite's descendants. Winchester streets might still be mudholes in the winter, the water supply might still be flowing from the spring through a log pipe, but the town had two newspapers, three schools, and five taverns. When in 1788 the Virginia Convention voted on the federal Constitution, the Shenandoah Valley cast its fourteen votes solidly for ratification.

Route 251, Effinger,
Rockbridge County

At the Black Horse Inn one evening, some young men were debating the merits of the Christian religion. An old man who had driven up in a shabby gig listened quietly while they argued from six in the evening until nine. Finally one of them laughingly asked him for his opinion. The quiet old gentleman sat up in his chair and spoke for an hour. He took each suggested point, summed it up, and gave a reasoned judgment. When the young men could break from their stunned silence, they ventured to ask his name. He was Chief Justice John Marshall, whose father had once been county clerk at Woodstock.

Visitors to the Shenandoah in the late-eighteenth and early-nineteenth century found life there stable and agreeable, but the sons and grandsons of the pioneers, moved by the classic American restlessness, began to seek their future farther west, and many who left the Valley were such men as make history. A Valley boy, John Sevier, founded Tennessee. A Valley boy, Sam Houston, founded Texas. Such familiar names as Bryan, Boone (who married a Valley girl, Rebecca Bryan), Lincoln, and Bowman were carried to Kentucky by the sons of Valley families.

The two great strains in American life, the pioneer and the homebuilder, were nowhere more mingled than in the Shenandoah Valley during the half century when the great roads to the Southwest ran

Cave Mountain Lake Recreation Area of the Jefferson National Forest, Rockbridge County

through it. Spirit and enterprise went from the Valley westward, as also did a ruthless and unruly element, and as they moved away the temper of the people gradually approximated the serenity of the landscape. In the first fifty years of the nineteenth century, the region of the Shenandoah lost forever all resemblance to its pioneering days.

The War of 1812 was fought far from the Valley, but again her people raised regiments and sent them into battle. A depression preceded the war, and inflation followed it. Still the Valley continued to grow, not suddenly, not due to booms or mineral wealth, but slowly, steadily, continually, as a tree grows in rich soil.

Washington Irving visited the Kennedys at Cassilis and wrote his name on Nellie Custis' door at Audley. He called the Shenandoah "a glorious valley, inhabited by an infinitely superior people."

The Indians were remote, the British back on the other side of the Atlantic, the French transformed by the mysterious alchemy of time into friends and allies. No one believed that the tranquil fields might ever again be the scene of organized murder.

CHAPTER 10

Inventions

Some had industrial ambitions for the Valley, hopes of improving the navigation of the river, where barges—"gundalows," to the lusty, gusty rivermen who rode them—regularly floated down but could not be poled back up; hopes, too, of large-scale smelting of the iron ore found in the mountains.

The Valley ore was indeed mined and smelted for a hundred years, but even though moderately profitable, it made no millionaires and created no industrial overdevelopment. The ore was not rich enough, the river was not deep enough; the way of the Valley was to give slowly—never great wealth, but competence, peace of heart, and time: time for people to develop what lay within them.

To Shepherdstown, shortly after the Revolution, came a man possessed by a dream of a boat that would move against the current without oars or sail. The neighbors called him "Crazy Rumsey." James Rumsey persisted. In 1784 he showed a model to George Washington. Armed with a testimonial, Rumsey secured from the Virginia legislature an exclusive right to construct and navigate boats on Virginia waters for ten years. He began actual work in the summer of 1785.

Not until 1787 was he ready, and so confident that he invited the public to witness the demonstration. A friend took the helm, another assisted with the engine, the fire burned brightly under the boiler, and James Rumsey set the machinery into noisy motion. After a breathless moment the boat began to chug upstream. General Gates tore off his hat and shouted, "My God! She moves!"

Move she did, upstream and down for two hours at an average rate of three miles an hour. They called it the "flying boat." A week later, even though the pipes had frozen, burst, and been wrapped with rags, Rumsey got her up to four miles an hour. Then he set off in triumph for Philadelphia to seek fame and fortune.

In 1792 he was preparing for a trial of his boat in England, when he died suddenly of a cerebral hemorrhage. A few weeks later the *Columbian Maid* moved successfully up the Thames without her inventor. There the matter ended except for a gold medal awarded to Rumsey's son in 1839 and a monument that still stands near Shepherdstown. Although Rumsey invented his steamboat—which actually used a rudimentary form of jet propulsion—long before Robert Fulton's famed success, today his name is little remembered.

Thirty years later, at the other end of the Valley, another and luckier inventor lived. In 1832 nineteen-year-old Cyrus McCormick began tinkering with a mechanical reaper his father had tried unsuccessfully to make. No one but Cyrus took it seriously. He kept on tinkering, assisted by a slave, Joe Anderson. Eight years passed before young McCormick felt ready to make a public demonstration in a neighbor's oatfield. He had the luck to arrive at exactly the right historical moment. The great west, the lush bottoms of the Ohio, the Missouri, and the Mississippi were opened. The reaper took hold at once.

Route 637 near Monterey, Highland County

For several years, Cyrus McCormick made the machines at home, selling as many as he could turn out. Then he realized that most of the demand came from the West and that since transportation was difficult, he should establish himself nearer his customers. In 1848 he moved to Chicago and there built up one of the historic American fortunes. A native of a slave state assisted by a slave, he had liberated the coming generations of farm labor by his invention.

And then there was Maury—Matthew Fontaine Maury (1806–1873), a descendant of that Fontaine who so obligingly kept a diary of Governor Spotswood's trip. A naval officer with a knee injury that retired him to the Department of Charts and Instruments at the Observatory in Washington, Maury became the "Pathfinder of the Seas," originating the signal service and making the first reliable charts of winds and currents, by means of which voyages under sail could be shortened by as much as 20 percent. Foreign governments recognized his work, decorated him, imitated his system, but he was lost to the United States Navy when, like so many others, he felt that he could not fight against Virginia.

The history of the Shenandoah Valley's contribution to the Industrial Revolution would not be complete without a mention of James Gibbs, a Connecticut Yankee living in Rockbridge County, who with his partner Wilcox became famous for his improved sewing machine. Gibbs was in business in the North when the Civil War broke out, but he came back to throw in his lot with his adopted people of Virginia. He would have shared their ruin had not his sewing machines gone on making money, so that at the end of the fighting he found $10,000 in his account in Philadelphia.

Cyrus McCormick's workshop, Steeles Tavern, Augusta County. McCormick worked here from 1832 to 1840 perfecting his mechanical reaper, which revolutionized farming and created one of America's great fortunes. His shop and farm are well preserved.

Buffalo Creek, near Effinger, Rockbridge County

Route 251,
Rockbridge County

*Gravel Spring Cemetery,
Gravel Springs, Frederick
County*

*Slave quarters, Mount
Pleasant, Buffalo Forge,
Rockbridge County. Now
owned by Pat and Douglas
Brady, Mount Pleasant was
once known as Meeting
House Plantation.*

*R*uin in the Valley seemed impossible in the comfortable 1850s, when the small houses had settled maturely among their groves. Belle Grove, Rion Hall, Carter Hall, Claymont, Linden Spring, Media, Saratoga, Graystone, Flowing Spring—in most instances the names were more pretentious than the houses.

Young ladies learned to ride in spite of corsets. They did not learn to walk, and those who had slaves did not learn to cook. Young gentlemen rode hard and well, shot straight, and were touchy on points of honor. They went to study at the University of Virginia, Washington College, VMI, Princeton, or West Point. Then they came home to manage their farms.

Yet there was a shadow on the land. No one would recognize its presence, still less admit it as a threat. Nevertheless a reckoning would be required. There were comparatively few slaves along the Shenandoah. Only 24 percent of the families even in wealthy Jefferson County owned slaves, and ten to a family was considered a large number. In the upper Valley, the proportion of blacks to whites was far lower. The Germans never considered it economical to own slaves, and many Quakers were outright abolitionists. As early as 1832, Augusta County elected a pro-emancipation legislator. Many slaves were allowed to buy their freedom, many were freed in wills.

It was not nearly enough, of course. The injustices of the system lay deeper than any court could reach, deeper than pride, too deep to be watered by the thin dew of occasional mercy. Too deep the gulf between master and slave for any of these—too deep, too wide, and filled with blood and fire.

CHAPTER 11

The Fateful Lightning

In the summer of 1860 a professor from the Virginia Military Institute in Lexington, a Major Thomas Jonathan Jackson, went north to take his usual cure for the "nervousness and cold feet" that afflicted him. Of the northerners he met, he wrote his sister Laura that "it is painful to discover with what unconcern they talk of war and threaten it."

The town of Harpers Ferry tumbles down steep streets to a roaring junction of the Shenandoah and the Potomac. Today it is the meeting point of three states, Maryland, Virginia, and West Virginia, but in 1858 West Virginia did not yet exist. Harpers Ferry was the link connecting the Valley and the West by rail and water to the world of cities and commerce. Along the Potomac and across a railroad bridge ran the Baltimore and Ohio Railroad, and the long low buildings of the United States Armory and Arsenal covered the flat beside the river.

In June of 1858 a young man from Connecticut came to Harpers Ferry, boarded with a widow, and married her daughter. He was, he said, a book agent, and his name was John Edwin Cook. The young and slender Mr. Cook spent a desultory year in book selling around the countryside. At Beall-Air, home

Harpers Ferry, West Virginia, with the Shenandoah River branching to the left of the picture and the Potomac to the right. Here John Brown staged his famous 1859 raid, hoping to ignite a slave rebellion.

Harpers Ferry. The B & O Railroad tunnel opened a vital link to the east. The first train arrived in 1834, having covered the eighty-two miles from Baltimore in six hours. As a railhead at a river junction, the town was a natural trade center and became a strategic location in the Civil War.

of Colonel Lewis Washington, he took a particular interest in the colonel's family heirloom, a sword presented to his illustrious uncle by Frederick the Great and inscribed, "From the oldest general in the world to the greatest."

In the summer of 1859 some other strangers came to the Valley, an elderly bearded man with piercing eyes who said that his name was Isaac Smith and that the three young men with him were his sons. They rented a remote farm five miles north of Harpers Ferry. By freight and wagon they brought in a large number of cases filled with "mining instruments."

The three months at the secluded farm must have been a difficult time for the eighteen other men hidden in the attic. Their leader was a burning man, as dangerous as a sharpened axe. John Brown had been a farmer, tanner, a preacher, who never succeeded in the worldly life, but had been called into the work of abolition. He had a price on his head in Kansas, where he had killed five men. He had escaped, grown a beard, and changed his name to Isaac Smith.

Now in the foothills of the Blue Ridge, he slowly collected and concealed more than two hundred rifles and a thousand pikes. His men came singly, by night, and were never seen about the farm in daylight. His was no casual hurried plot, but long formulated and carefully worked out. At Chatham, in

Canada, Brown and his friends had met and drawn up a new Constitution of the United States with himself as commander in chief, with a cabinet, a Congress, but no Senate.

On the night of Sunday, October 16, John Brown led his well-armed followers to Harpers Ferry. They left three to guard the farmhouse. Without firing a shot, they took prisoner the watchman at the armory, the watchman at the railroad bridge, the watchman at Hall's Rifle Works, half a mile up the River, and established themselves in those buildings. Then John Cook and others went to the home of Colonel Washington and took him hostage with his sword, pistols, and some slaves. In the same way another band took John Allstadt and others, and brought them in a wagon to John Brown.

"I am Osawatommie Brown of Kansas," he told the hostages and buckled on Washington's sword. He gave pikes to the slaves and told them to stand guard over their masters. What could he have hoped for when he and his handful seized government property? Was it to be a general slave uprising that would enthrone him while an aroused North rushed to his assistance? The answer is lost. Lost in the windowless darkness of the slave cabins. How much preparation had Brown made among the slaves themselves? No one knows, no one will ever know. Not one slave rose.

The raiders killed one man on Sunday night, a free man of color, the station porter, Shepherd Hayward, who saw them stop the Wheeling Express on the bridge at midnight and walked out to see what had happened. After a short delay the raiders let the Express go, and when the news reached Washington a detachment of marines was promptly ordered to Harpers Ferry. In the meantime, local militia—the Hamtramck Guards from Shepherdstown and the Jefferson Guards and Jefferson Volunteers—surrounded the armory but made no frontal attacks. They did dislodge the small group occupying the Rifle Works, drove them into the river, and shot them down.

As Monday wore on, however, the hopelessness of the raider's position became more and more obvious. The bodies of four townsmen now lay across the path to peace—including old Mayor Beckham, shot as he went forward unarmed and alone to stop the bloodshed in his peaceful town.

Night fell. There was no light inside the armory's little engine house, to which Brown had withdrawn. At eleven o'clock, he sent one of his prisoners to ask that the raiders be allowed to withdraw across the bridge into Maryland. No truce. No terms. His mortally wounded son Oliver cried in the darkness, "Kill me and put me out of this suffering."

"If you must die," said John Brown, "die like a man."

It was a long, black, seemingly endless night. The marines arrived under the command of Colonel Robert E. Lee and replaced the militia around the armory. At dawn, Lee ordered Lieutenant J. E. B. Stuart to take twelve men to the door of the engine house and demand surrender, with a promise of protection from the mob. Brown offered the counterproposal that his men be allowed the length of the bridge as a start for escape. Colonel Lee ordered the marines to break down the door.

All the fighting was over in three minutes. One marine was killed, one wounded. Two more raiders were dead. The rest were taken outside and their wounds dressed. The hostages came out, dazed, hungry, recovering from their fright and breathing deep drafts of the sparkling October morning.

John Brown and the survivors were taken to the Charles Town jail to await trial. Of his twenty-two men, ten had been killed and five had escaped.

John Brown may have hoped to precipitate a national issue, to involve the central government, to start a war. His northern backers were loud in their disavowals of such a plan. Few protested when he

*Stone steps leading
to St. Peter's Church and
Jefferson Rock, Harpers Ferry*

was tried in a Virginia court. They held a fair trial in Charles Town, as even Brown admitted in his last speech. The facts spoke for themselves and the verdict could not be in doubt. The court sentenced Brown to hang on December 2.

John Brown passed his last month quietly, writing letters full of allusions to the sword of the Lord and Gideon, which fell like sparks on the tinder of the North. He had a lively appreciation of his value as a martyr and refused all offers of rescue. "I am worth infinitely more now to die than to live," he said. "I can regain all of the ground lost by merely hanging a few minutes by the neck."

On December 1 he was visited by his wife, mother of the four sons who had all been killed in following him. To her, John Brown gave his last written message: "I, John Brown, am now quite *certain* that the crimes of *this guilty land:* will never be purged *away:* but with Blood."

The morning of December 2 dawned misty sweet. John Brown, in a rusty black frock coat and red carpet slippers, stood for a moment on the threshold of the jail. "This is a beautiful country," said Brown to the undertaker. "I have never had the pleasure of seeing it before."

John Brown's body swung into eternity, and into a marching song.

Muscovy duck, North Fork,
Warren County

I see before me now a travelling army halting,

Below, a fertile Valley spaced with barns and the orchards of summer,

Behind, the terraced sides of a mountain, abrupt, in places rising high,

Broken with rocks, with clinging cedars, with tall shapes dingily seen.

The numerous campfires scattered near and far, some away up on a mountain,

The shadowy forms of men and horses, looming, large sized, flickering,

And over all the sky—the sky! far, far out of reach, studded, breaking out,

* the eternal stars.*

—Walt Whitman

CHAPTER 12

The Swift Sword

The people of the Shenandoah Valley did not want war, could not believe that it would come, watched it approach with dread. In the Valley, slaves were never more than 10 percent of the population. When delegates were elected for the Virginia Convention in February, 1861, every county in the Valley sent only Union delegates. On April 4 the Convention rejected secession by a vote of 85 to 45. On April 12 Fort Sumter was fired upon. On April 15 President Lincoln called for 75,000 volunteers. Virginia could not be exempted from raising her share, and troops were to be sent across her to hold the Deep South in check. On April 17 her Convention adopted the Ordinance of Secession. And in every hamlet in the Valley, companies of volunteers began to form.

To understand these apparent inconsistencies, one thing should be remembered. Within the memories of the fathers of these men was a time when there had been no Union. A united country was a new thing, a fine thing, a dream not three-quarters of a century old. There had been a Virginia for nearly 250 years.

At VMI that angular professor of mathematics, Major Jackson, summed it up with his usual terseness: "I am in favor of making a thorough trial for peace, and if we fail in this and the State is invaded, to defend it with a terrific resistance."

Major Jackson was ordered to bring the cadet corps of VMI to the army in Richmond. Look closely at this Major Jackson, for he and the Valley were to achieve their immortality together. He was not born there, but he adopted it. He loved it enough to fight for it.

A trans-Allegheny boy, an orphan from the rough-and-ready foothills between the mountains and the Ohio, he had gone to West Point late, self-educated, and had crawled by hard study from the foot of his class to graduate seventeenth. George B. McClellan won all the laurels, but someone noticed the lanky mountaineer and remarked: "If we had to stay here another year, Old Jack would be at the head of the class."

In the war with Mexico, Jackson did well enough to become a major within eighteen months. After that war he was offered the post of professor of natural and experimental philosophy at VMI. From the age of twenty-six to thirty-six he lived quietly at Lexington. He joined the Presbyterian Church and resigned his soul completely to God as his commander.

As a teacher, Old Jack was not a qualified success. His students found his eccentricities amusing, his punctiliousness funny. In his home life, he laid aside the caution with which he faced the world, and his wife has left a biography of a gentle, tender husband, whose strongest rebuke was, "Ah, that is not the way to be happy," and who called her "My little sunshine."

Sherando Lake Recreation Area, Augusta County, in fall

When Virginia seceded, Major Jackson was promoted to colonel and sent to command the garrison of Virginia Volunteers at Harpers Ferry—"the post I prefer above all others," he wrote his wife. He was resolved by discipline and drill to make an army out of the eight thousand motley volunteers who had poured in from the surrounding countryside.

Over the B & O Railroad, then the only link between Washington and the pro-Union western Virginia, an unprecedented number of coal cars were rolling to the capital. Jackson informed the president of the road that the traffic disturbed his camp at night and must stop. Then he said that the daylight traffic interfered with military routine, and that all freights must run exclusively between the hours of eleven A.M. and one P.M. Again the railroad complied. Jackson sent Captain Imboden of Staunton across the Potomac at Harpers Ferry to stop the east-bound freights and let the west-bound go through. The officer in charge at Martinsburg was ordered to act on the opposite principle. The trap closed, and in an hour the Virginians had scooped up fifty-six locomotives and more than three hundred cars.

Belle Boyd's house in Front Royal, where she lived for part of the war. The Confederate spy was celebrated for her courage and resourcefulness.

Despite this coup, Jackson was relieved of his command the very next day and superseded by General Joseph E. Johnston; President Jefferson Davis wished to place a more experienced officer at this important post. Jackson was retained at Harpers Ferry, promoted to brigadier general, and given the First Brigade of Virginians in Johnston's army, a brigade largely composed of Valley men.

Within three weeks Federal general Patterson arrived from Washington with a considerable force. As Harpers Ferry was untenable, the Confederates fell back to Winchester. When Patterson advanced to Martinsburg, Jackson was there before him to burn almost all of the railroad cars and forty-two of the locomotives he had so recently bottled up, and to haul the rest with horses down the Valley Pike to the branch lines, where they became very useful.

May and June were gay in Winchester—apple blossoms and uniforms, roses and swords. This was the romantic, the traditional Virginia, the legend deeply believed, where all the girls were beautiful and all the men were brave. The war could not last long, for the Yankees did not like fighting, everyone said. The newborn nation would be rich and free; what they lacked in ammunition they made up in dash and spirit. Everywhere there were young laughing soldiers, volunteers and eager. Hostesses set three or four supper tables every night. The ladies sewed night and day making havelocks—which turned out to be perfectly useless—and haversacks, jackets, trousers, even tents. As for the young girls, they were in paradise. When it was all over, one of them could look back at her sixteen-year-old self flirting there in the moonlight and still say, "The girls of this generation will never know the good times we had then."

The new Confederate army had time to laugh, for there was still no serious fighting. (In a small skirmish, which the generals referred as "that little affair at Falling Waters," Colonel J. E. B. Stuart captured a scouting company of Federals. It gave the Confederate trooper a good opinion of himself, and only one of them got hurt.)

There were Yankees at Martinsburg and Yankees at Harpers Ferry. When General Patterson occupied Martinsburg on July 3 there were many northern sympathizers in town, but one young woman emphatically was not. Belle Boyd, all of sixteen, was living in the home of her childhood, a two-storied house overgrown with roses and honeysuckle. Her father had gone off as a private in the Confederate army, and her mother, never alone since marrying at fifteen, was suitably prostrated. On Independence Day the Yankee troops, celebrating with the benefit of whiskey, came to the Boyd home to confiscate the Rebel flags with which Miss Belle had decorated her room. The soldiers insisted that they were going to raise a Union flag over the house, and Mrs. Boyd, with her little children clinging to her skirts in the classic pose, retorted that she and every member of her family would die first. One of the soldiers then spoke to her insultingly. Belle drew a pistol from her bosom and shot him dead.

The comrades of the dead man would have burned the house had not Miss Belle sent a message to the commanding officer. He came in person to investigate, told Belle that she had done "just right," and placed sentries around the house to see that the family was not molested further. Miss Belle made friends with the sentries and the young officers who came to inquire for "the little Rebel with the chestnut curls"—and stole their pistols, swords, and bullets, which she smuggled through the lines together with such information as she could gather. One dispatch was intercepted, her handwriting identified, and General Patterson summoned her to his headquarters. The general was displeased. He spoke severely to her and went so far as to read her the Articles of War. "Miss Boyd," said the general, "I positively forbid

Our Cemetery, final resting place for 500 Confederate soldiers, Mount Jackson, Shenandoah County

Autumn leaves, Skyline Drive

you to do anything of this sort again." Her spirits might have remained chastened for a time had not the victory at Bull Run revived them.

At dawn on July 18 the people of Winchester heard the tramping and came out with pale and wondering faces to see their army deserting them. The line stretched for seven miles down the pike, at its head General Jackson in the faded uniform he had brought from VMI, mounted on his close-coupled, uninspiring, tireless horse, Little Sorrel. They were going to Manassas. The cheers rolled back down the line. They marched all day. At dusk they forded the Shenandoah with the cool water curling about their waists and climbed the Blue Ridge in the twilight, shoulders rubbed sore under the haversacks, dust caked into mud, muskets growing heavier no matter how they were carried. The column reached the crest and wound through Ashby's Gap and down the other side. It was two in the morning, and the two-month soldiers had marched twenty miles. An officer came up to General Jackson.

"The men are all asleep. Shall I rouse someone for picket duty?"

"Let the poor fellows sleep. I will watch the camp myself."

Back in the Valley suddenly empty and quiet, the people waited. Friday, Saturday, and Sunday passed without news. Then on Monday all the bells were ringing, ringing for victory. It had been glorious. It had been wonderful. It had been just as they expected. The Yankees had run all the way to Washington, they were the "Bull Runners" sure enough, and the war was nearly over.

But on Tuesday the wagons began rolling back bearing the fruits of victory—"the first fruits of that bitter tree which our people had helped to plant and nourish." Here were the bloody, groaning wounded, the stiff and livid figures under the motionless tarpaulins.

The people of the Valley were changed forever. They would never again talk with the same glibness and assurance of the future, for they had learned the first lesson of many lessons.

War is not drill and flags, cheering and gallantry. War is death.

There is Jackson, standing like a stone wall.
Rally behind the Virginians.
—General Bee at Manassas

CHAPTER 13

Marching On

General Jackson and his brigade won a new name at Manassas.

To his wife, after reminding her that all the glory was due to God alone, Jackson permitted himself to be expansive: "He made my brigade more instrumental than any other in repulsing the main attack."

In October he was promoted to major general and ordered to the Valley in charge of the new Shenandoah District. To his mind this had only one defect: he must leave his Stonewall Brigade behind. He bade them an emotional farewell, but within a month brigade and general were together in the Valley, never to separate while he lived.

In the North after Manassas, they stopped talking about "thirty days of concerted effort" and men poured into the Federal army at the rate of 40,000 a month; but in the South a tenth of the troops went home on leave, sure now that they could lick twice their weight in Yankees.

In Winchester the townspeople were beginning to find some drawbacks to having an army camped at their doors, but they did not complain so long as it was the right army. Miss Boyd tried six weeks of nursing and found it undermining to her health.

General Jackson had no intention of wasting the winter. Since his government would not support an expedition to western Virginia, he determined to take Romney, a town just over the first range of the Alleghenies, thereby securing the Valley and the B & O Railroad.

Bushong Farm, New Market Battlefield, Shenandoah County. Here, in one of the war's legendary episodes, boy cadets from the Virginia Military Institute marched out to fight side by side with veteran Confederate troops against a larger Union force.

He started west on New Year's Day. Then the snow began to fall. Next day it turned to ice, and the wagons skidded so that four men with ropes had to hold each one in the road. By night the snow fell soft and thick, resting like wool on the blankets of the exhausted men. A group of them in a shivering huddle kept themselves warm by cursing their commander. Old Jack was crazy, he was trying to kill them, nobody could be expected to stand this kind of thing. At dawn an angular soldier rose from beside them, brushed off the snow, bade them a courteous good morning and strode away. It was Jackson.

For ten days the Army of the Valley toiled on. The Federals kept retreating before them, and Romney was empty when they arrived. Jackson left General Loring in charge and took the rest of his army back to the Valley. On January 24 he reached Winchester. General Loring did not like his position, complained to Richmond over Jackson's head, and without consulting Jackson, Richmond ordered Romney evacuated.

Jackson wrote a letter of resignation to Secretary of War Benjamin. The resignation was not passed over in silence. Many important people protested. In the end, after a solemn assurance that the government would never again interfere with his military plans, General Jackson was preserved for the army.

In March, General Johnston, Confederate commander in chief, took stock of his position and decided to evacuate Manassas and fall back nearer to Richmond. Now Jackson was unsupported. His army numbered 4,600. Across the Potomac, Banks waited with 37,000. Frémont at Romney had 12,000 more, and Jackson looked like a small mouse in a closing trap. Confronted by the possibility of immediate action, his twin plagues of nervousness and cold feet left him entirely. He began his retreat by marching in the direction of the enemy, in the hope of tempting Banks to give him battle. But Banks was cautious.

On March 12, Jackson ordered his army to move south. He summoned a council of his regimental officers and disclosed his plans. He intended to bring his troops back into Winchester under the cover of darkness and to make a surprise attack on the Federals. The regimental officers felt that they could not be brought back in time and voted solidly to give up the attempt.

Cedar Creek Battlefield, Middletown, Frederick County. In October of 1864, a rout of Union forces by General ~~Mosby~~ EARLY brought General Sheridan flying from Kernsville to rally his men and crush the Confederates.

Thus, with a retreat before overwhelming forces, Stonewall Jackson began the Valley Campaign that would make him famous. Accompanied by his surgeon, Dr. McGuire, Jackson halted on the southern ridge of Winchester for one last look. The town lay quiet under the newly feathered branches of its trees. Dr. McGuire wrote, "Jackson's face was fairly blazing with the fire of wrath that was burning in him. . . . I felt awed before him. Presently he cried out in a tone almost savage: 'That is the last council of war I will ever hold.'"

It was a promise that he kept.

A defensive campaign can only be made
successful by taking the offensive at
the proper time.
—T. J. Jackson

CHAPTER 14

The Invaded

The angry general on the hill below Winchester did not come to his great trial unprepared. He had accurate maps drawn of the Valley from Harpers Ferry to Lexington, and he studied them. The country boy who had made a man of himself by hard work and determination was not neglecting any advantage that hard work could provide. He made the countryside his ally, the rolling fields edged with woodland, the streams swollen with spring, the hidden roads, the friendly houses, and above all the great shaggy bulk of Massanutten, splitting the Valley in two, crossed by secret paths.

In justice one thing must be stated. In spite of the ruin this war brought upon the Valley, in spite of its horrendous casualties, unsurpassed in the nation's history, it was by modern standards a gentle war. The soldiers themselves were the first to discover it as they swapped tobacco for coffee across the river.

On the morning after Jackson's men withdrew, the people of Winchester woke to sunlight and silence. Then from the distance they heard martial music. The children jumped up shouting, "Our men are coming back!" "Wait," said the mothers. There was no mistaking it. It was "The Star-Spangled Banner" that the bands were playing. The newly arrived army wore crisp blue uniforms very different from the homespun and individualistic headgear that had just departed, but these too were American boys from no very distant states. Most of them had been raised on farms not unlike farms in the Valley.

Colonel Lewis Moore's home, Winchester. Stonewall Jackson used the house as his headquarters during 1861 and 1862.

The people of this occupied territory were still proud, unpacified, and indignant. Their houses were subject to search or seizure, their chickens disappeared, sometimes a horse was stolen. "When we had a closer acquaintance with war, we wondered how such things could have disturbed us so much."

When the cautious General Banks discovered how few men Jackson had, he sent General Shields with 11,000 to catch him and prepared to withdraw his main body to Washington. On March 22, Jackson's little army marched twenty-two miles, the next morning—Sunday—fourteen more. This brought them to Kernstown, a village four miles south of Winchester, by one o'clock.

The Yankees stretched over the gentle ridges on either side of the Valley Pike. Between the enemies lay freshly plowed fields, wet from the spring thaw, fenced with rails and a few stone walls. They could see each other plainly, and Jackson believed that he had all the enemy in view. If he waited, Union reinforcements might come up. At half past three he gave the order to attack. Within fifteen minutes the gray soldiers had seized the ridge. Then suddenly a roar of musketry burst in their faces, and hidden Union regiments leapt out. Jackson saw with astonishment his Stonewall Brigade in retreat. General Garnett had given the order. There was nothing to do but count the day lost.

Twilight fell. Through the night lumbered the wagons of Dr. McGuire, carrying the wounded to the rear.

Not until after the Federal casualties had been cared for could the people of Winchester make their pilgrimage to the bloodstained fields near Kernstown. The churches, the banks, the courthouses were turned into hospitals. On the courthouse porch lay rows of dead men with papers pinned to them telling who they had been.

A long April and May passed in Winchester. The blue soldiers came and went, the people waited for news and heard nothing. Where was the Army of the Shenandoah? Again spring came. What man had destroyed, grass and rain made new. The soft blades laid a tender velvet over the scars, bloom frosted the mock orange and syringa.

"It was the last look of beauty that scene ever wore," wrote a Winchester diarist who hoped to keep her home for her eight children. She described how the northerners had taken over the place after bringing in a young officer who had broken his leg. When she came down in the morning her house was unrecognizable, for coats, saddles, and equipment were drying everywhere and the colors in the carpets had disappeared under the mud. Having cleared the dining room, she forced her way into the kitchen and in an hour had breakfast ready for her family.

The people of the lower Valley had great faith, but they began to feel as had one soldier when he looked down from Henry Hill at First Manassas and saw the distant meadows blue with Union troops.

"My God, have we still got all them to fight?"

If I can deceive my friends I can be
sure of deceiving the enemy.
—T. J. Jackson

CHAPTER 15

Valley Campaign I

The course of the war after Kernstown showed that General Jackson had some reason for satisfaction. General Shields was convinced that Jackson would not have ventured so boldly if he had not had a large force ready to reinforce him. Banks hastily reversed his eastward march and returned to the Valley. Thus McClellan on the eve of attacking Richmond found his army reduced and his operation suspended. All this Stonewall Jackson had accomplished with an effective force of about 4,600, of whom he had lost a fourth.

The Confederate Congress passed a resolution thanking him. Jackson court-martialed Garnett for ordering the retreat without instructions and relieved him of command. By March 29, McClellan had ordered Banks to drive Jackson from the Valley. When Banks at last advanced, on April 17, Jackson fell back to a new camp at Conrad's Store, a crossroads near Swift Run Gap. There he completed the reorganization of his army under the new Conscription Act. Officers were elected for the last time, after which they were to be appointed for merit only. If Jackson had a plan, he confided it to no one. His uncomfortable position was strategically sound, for from it he might cross the Blue Ridge and join Ewell in eastern Virginia, or he might reenter the Valley by one of three roads.

On April 30, General Jackson ordered Ewell to come through Swift Run Gap and occupy the camp

Elizabeth Iron Furnace, Route 717 near Basye, Shenandoah County. Furnaces like this one, scattered throughout the Valley, provided shot and cannon for the Confederacy.

at Conrad's Store as long as Banks was in the Valley. He sent cavalry, commanded by the soon-to-be-legendary Turner Ashby, to annoy Banks. Then for no reason that anyone could see, he marched the remainder of his army over sixteen miles of the most bottomless road in Virginia, to the village of Port Republic. As soon as they arrived they promptly swung back toward the mountains. Now the army knew that their general was crazy, for they had camped only twelve miles from this spot three days before.

"Always mystify, mislead and surprise the enemy," Jackson said.

At the eastern foot of the mountains the soldiers climbed aboard trains. Now they knew that they were going to defend Richmond. But the trains went back to Staunton. The unprotected citizens of Staunton, fearfully waiting for the invader, were overjoyed when their defenders rolled into town on Sunday, May 4. Then a disturbing rumor began to circulate that Jackson did not intend to defend the town. A deputation of prominent citizens called upon him to discover the truth of it. Jackson pulled their leader into a private conference.

"Judge Baldwin, can you keep a secret?"

"Certainly, general. Certainly."

"Well, so can I."

On Tuesday the Army of the Valley marched out of Staunton to the west. They climbed a mountain range, this time the Alleghenies. When they had carried their knapsacks for twenty miles, they were ordered to pile them in a village street and to advance on the double. Now they knew that Old Jack had work for them to do, and the knowledge stimulated them. After a march of twenty-six miles they found a small Confederate force under "Allegheny" Johnson engaging the troops of Milroy, one of Frémont's generals, on the craggy mountain slopes around the village of McDowell. This was the battle where they set the woods on fire.

Memorial erected in 1905 by surviving members of the Union's 54th Pennsylvania Volunteer Infantry, Route 11 north of New Market, Shenandoah County

The Rebels held the mountaintops, and the Yankees from Ohio and West Virginia clambered up like wildcats, were thrown back, clambered up again. Night fell, and under the cover of darkness the Union army withdrew. For three days Jackson pursued them through the burning woods, then rested his army half a day to hold a service of thanksgiving. (Whenever his men missed a Sunday at church due to military necessity, "Old Bluelight" tried to make it up during the week and in this manner sometimes celebrated three Sundays in three days.)

Meanwhile, General Ewell, left with the barest of orders, sat in camp at Swift Run Gap fuming—and did not care who knew it. On April 14, however, a courier brought encouragement: Jackson had started back to the Valley, and Ewell should attack Banks. This was welcome news, but before Ewell could act, the supreme command ordered him to return to Richmond. He got into the saddle and rode a day and a night to tell Jackson what had happened.

"Then Providence denies me the privilege of striking a decisive blow for my country," Jackson said.

Ewell, famously an agnostic, did not see what Providence had to do with it, but as he listened to the man whom he had called "that enthusiastic fanatic," he began to see something more in him. The two agreed that a blow at Winchester and a threat to Washington would disturb President Lincoln more than a few additional thousands in the vastly outnumbered garrison at Richmond, and Ewell bravely decided to risk his military career by delaying until Jackson could telegraph Lee and receive a reply. When a favorable reply came back, the two generals began a working partnership that was to prove eminently successful.

Ewell's command joined Jackson's at Harrisonburg on the evening of May 20 after three long marches. General Taylor's Louisianians, French Creoles who marched to waltz time, wheeled into camp as jauntily as if they had been on parade, and Taylor found his new commander sitting on a fence sucking a lemon.

"How far have you come today?" asked Jackson in a low and gentle voice.

"Six and twenty miles."

"You seem to have no stragglers."

"I never allow straggling, General."

"You must teach my men, they straggle badly."

The next day in the gray of the morning, the Army of the Valley moved north, 17,000 strong. For the first time Stonewall commanded a considerable force, and at once he put their faith in him to a severe test. Instead of going up the Pike to attack Banks at Strasburg, they swung right, crossed Massanutten, and vanished into the Luray Valley.

If Jackson's friends were confused, the enemy was more so. McDowell reported from the Rappahannock that Jackson was in front of him. Schenck, in the Alleghenies, said that Jackson was at his rear. Frémont, in West Virginia, reported that Jackson was going west. Banks felt sure that he was still in Harrisonburg. President Lincoln dryly remarked that when a force got that badly strung out, it should be possible to hit it somewhere in the middle and cut it in two.

On May 22, Banks wrote a placid dispatch to the president. "I regard it as certain that Jackson will move north as far as New Market. . . . He is obstinate in his intention to defend the Valley, but I see no cause for immediate alarm." In light of this conclusion, Banks decided that Shields should leave a garrison of 2,000 at Front Royal.

On that night, ten miles from Front Royal, within striking distance of the Valley Pike, Jackson was camping in the Federal rear.

CHAPTER 16

Valley Campaign II

*T*he Yankees ran from Front Royal but they did not run fast enough. The Rebels killed or captured 904 of the town's garrison of 1,063, and this with a loss of only 50 men. General Banks did not take the information seriously. Merely another cavalry raid.

At seven on the morning of May 24, Banks reported that Jackson was still in front of him on the Valley Pike, but by nine he had seen the light. He began to move and in a hurry. The Rebels were two miles nearer Winchester than he, on their way from Front Royal, but they were advancing slowly.

Still Jackson led his army down the Pike. Without lunch, without dinner. Darkness fell and brought no bivouac. Again the soldiers thought that someone had forgotten to halt them.

On and on through the black spring night, scuffling, dragging, heads down, shoulders bowed. About two o'clock an officer rode up to report that his men were falling beside the road, and unless he could rest them they would be ineffective for the inevitable battle in the morning.

"I am obliged to sweat them tonight that I may save their blood tomorrow," replied Jackson. "The line of hills below Winchester must not be occupied by the enemy."

But Stonewall was at last obliged to order two hours of rest two miles outside of town. The men dropped where they stood in the road, and slept. Jackson and Ashby tied their horses to a fence and paced

*Jeb Stuart's home, Staunton.
A dashing cavalry commander,
Stuart was the eyes and ears
of Lee's army. He was fatally
wounded in May of 1864.*

to and fro passing each other like silent sentinels, each absorbed in his own thoughts. Before two hours had passed, a faint gray tinged the black pool of the sky, and Jackson mounted to begin the day. He observed that in spite of every effort, the Federal guns had had time to take position on the hill.

"General Taylor, can your brigade charge a battery?"

"It can try."

"Very good. Move it forward."

Five terse words of command to General Winder and the Stonewall Brigade: "You must occupy that hill."

This was the battle, the screaming, bloody conclusion toward which they had plodded through the warm and secret night. Here were the sloping fields, the dew-drenched meadows where blood must wash away the dew. General Jackson covered the field in the blazing absorption that consumed him during an engagement, ignoring the bullets as if they were raindrops.

Charge and fire, fall and charge. Until at last the Yankees around the batteries wavered, then ran in panic down the hill. "Forward after the enemy!" shouted Jackson. "Tell the whole army to press forward to the Potomac."

On Little Sorrel he bounded up the ridge. Over the crest lay Winchester, and the general tore off his cap and yelled like any private. "Very good!" he shouted, then reverting to his native idiom, "Let's holler!"

*Quarter horses, Mountaintop
Ranch, Jollett, Page County*

The Yankees ran in complete confusion. "Never was there such a chance for cavalry!" cried Jackson. "Oh, that my cavalry were in place!" But the cavalry were missing. He ordered the artillery to unhitch their horses and pursue bareback, but it was plain that the half-dead animals had nothing left. About five miles north of Winchester Jackson ended the chase.

It was a sunny, quiet Sabbath evening, another Sunday battle, but this time "Old Bluelight" did not apologize, for Winchester was free. In three May weeks the Army of the Valley had marched 170 miles, routed three armies, seized supplies worth $125,185, accounted for a third of the enemy, and driven the Yankees across the Potomac—driven them out of the Valley.

General Banks put the best possible face on what he called "a premeditated march of near sixty miles in the face of the enemy," but Washington did not share his satisfaction in this strategic retreat. Only the ragged Rebels had a good word for the defeated general. Affectionately they called him "Commissary Banks." They feasted on lobster, cheese, canned peaches, piccolomini and candy, coffee, ale, and milk.

Five days they rested at Winchester. They were learning what every soldier learns—that in war everything that is done has to be done over, for no battle is decisive until the final battle. Now, although they were surrounded by 60,000 Union troops, they talked less about the "crazy" general. A new spirit pervaded the Army of the Valley.

"Old Jack got us into this fix, and with the blessing of God he will get us out of it."

Valley Campaign III

*W*inchester was to change hands more than threescore times before the war ended. It had a brief respite when General Jackson took it from General Banks. Happy as most people were, they had to curb their hospitality: food was not so plentiful as it had been, and many of the "servants" had gone off with the Yankees.

Jackson did not waste time resting in Winchester but sent the Stonewall Brigade to make a demonstration toward Harpers Ferry in the teeth of the Federal guns mounted on Maryland Heights. On the way back from Harpers Ferry, he heard that Front Royal had been retaken.

In this crisis, Jackson asked his friend A. R. Boteler to go to Richmond with a request for additional troops. With forty thousand men, he said, he could carry the war to the Susquehanna.

"What will you do, general, if they cut you off here?"

"Fall back on Maryland for reinforcements."

The retreat began. Before dawn the supply wagons started on another creaking and rumbling journey down the Valley Pike. Four thousand prisoners followed under guard, and then the army. Jackson sent word to the Stonewall Brigade at Harpers Ferry that he would try to wait for them, but if they could not come up in time, they must take to the mountains and join him later. He himself did not leave Winchester until the last soldier was gone.

Covered bridge, Meems Bottom, Shenandoah County. During the Valley Campaign, Jackson's army, retreating before oncoming Union forces, rested here after destroying the bridges to the north and to the south.

The army marched on with a ten-minute rest every hour, and every man urged to lie down flat while he was resting. When they reached Strasburg, Frémont was only three miles to the west. Ewell went to hold him while the wagon train proceeded. At Strasburg the Stonewall Brigade caught up after an all-night march of thirty-six miles.

Throughout another blustery night, Taylor, Winder, and Ashby kept the enemy at bay behind them. Jackson burned the bridges below New Market so that Shields could not surprise him by coming across Massanutten. He burned the bridges behind him at Meem's Bottom, and the Shenandoah rose to his assistance, flooding twelve feet in four hours and washing away the pontoons on which Frémont hoped to cross.

And now the soldiers had a respite of a day or two, while on the broad spreading meadows near Harrisonburg, Ashby and his men kept the vanguard of the Federals amused. By now Ashby had dared death so many times it seemed death did not want him. But in the last skirmish of the day, an unimportant little engagement without a name, a gallop at sunset through a field of golden wheat with Ashby at the head of it, his stallion was shot out from under him. He leapt up and ran forward, waving his sword, calling to his men to follow. A bullet struck his heart. His troopers fought wildly, drove off the enemy, and carried him back to camp sobbing like children. Jackson wrote a eulogy in his official report: "His daring was proverbial, his powers of endurance almost incredible, his character heroic, and his sagacity almost intuitive." All Virginia burst into tears and verse. Ashby was gone, and with him passed the last glory and romance of this war, leaving the long road of blood to be traveled under a burning sky to the end.

The morning of June 8 dawned blue and cloudless and brought another Sunday battle. General Jackson, in his headquarters on a hill outside of Port Republic, knew that Shields was coming after him down the Luray Valley and Frémont down the Main Valley, and that there would be no more dodging around Massanutten. But he still hoped to prevent a joining of the two forces. On his way to devotional exercises, he heard firing in the town below him. Almost immediately sounds of cannonading to the west announced that Ewell had already engaged Frémont at Cross Keys. Jackson waited, anticipating an attack from Shields. "Delightful excitement!" he said to General Taylor.

With or without the assistance of that Providence in which he did not believe, General Ewell repulsed the Federals because Frémont threw in his numerically superior troops too cautiously. Ewell rested on the field, where Jackson joined him. By two o'clock in the morning, Stonewall had his plans prepared and made ready to move again. He ordered Colonel Patton to hold Frémont in check while the rest of the army disposed of Shields.

But across the river at Port Republic, Jackson found Shields a more formidable opponent than he had expected. These men had whipped him once in the Valley, and they set their hearts on whipping him again. He began to see that he could not make his schedule. Reluctantly he ordered Patton to join him and to burn the bridge behind him. The fresh reinforcements made the Federals waver. After the hardest-fought and bloodiest battle of the campaign, the northerners finally retreated around twelve o'clock—two hours late. Jackson had to abandon his plan of going after Frémont.

Jackson had dealt with the two armies that were pursuing him, his wagon train was safe in the mountains at Brown's Gap, his prisoners had been sent south, his losses were comparatively few. With an army that had never exceeded 17,000, he had disposed of 30,000. In six weeks his men had marched 400 miles, defeated four armies, fought five battles (with skirmishes almost every day), captured 4,000 prisoners and compendious stores, held 175,000 men in two great armies immobile before Richmond and Petersburg. Rarely in the history of war has so much been accomplished by so few. After the battle of Port Republic, General Jackson laid his hand gently on the arm of the godless General Ewell.

"He who does not see the hand of God in this, is blind, sir. Blind!"

The Army of the Valley rested for five days. Then in such secrecy that even his staff did not know where he had gone, Jackson visited Richmond, consulted Lee, returned, and led his army east across the mountains. "If my coat knew my plans," he said, "I would take it off and burn it."

All quiet along the Potomac tonight,
Except here and there a stray picket
Is shot, as he walks on his beat to and fro,
By a rifleman hid in the thicket.
It is nothing. A private or two now and then,
Will not count in the news of the battle.
Not an officer lost, only one of the men,
Going out on a long death rattle.
—Ethel Lynn Beers, "All Quiet Along the Potomac"

CHAPTER 18

The Long Year

And now the Valley was again without its army. The two weeks of joy in Winchester fled like a dream, a confused time of troops passing and repassing, a chance to hear something of husbands, sons, or sweethearts, a time of wildly optimistic rumors. Then General Jackson withdrew, mysterious as ever, then the Yankees came back: Blenker's Brigade, the German Division, many of whom hardly spoke English, officered by Germans and with a German manner toward the inhabitants of occupied territory.

The homesick Valley men, the "foot cavalry" waded the Potomac and entered Maryland through country that reminded them of the Valley. Ragged, barefoot, dirty, they marched through Frederick.

The tide was high at Antietam, where with the Potomac at his back, Lee and forty thousand men gave battle to twice as many Federals, where in the reddened waters of the river flowed the blood of three thousand bodies toward the bay. Where twenty thousand Americans fell at the hands of their brothers. All the next day both armies waited, lying on their arms. McClellan did not attack, Lee could not. On the night of September 18, under a fine warm rain that thickened the darkness, the Confederates fell back into Virginia.

The summer campaign of 1862 had ended. It had begun on the Chickahominy, thirty miles from

Stonewall Jackson keeps watch from the Barracks at VMI, Lexington.

Richmond; it ended on the Potomac sixty miles from Washington. For a month the armies lay inactive, looking at each other, and it was all quiet along the river. There was not a Yankee left in Virginia.

The patient Mr. Lincoln, who had been disappointed in so many generals, said that the South must have a million men under arms, for every time his troops engaged the Rebel army it was reported that they had encountered twice their strength—and he knew the North had half a million.

On his way back from Maryland, General Jackson was mobbed by the liberated ladies of Martinsburg, who strewed his path with roses, cut the buttons from his coat, and threatened to have his hair. He escaped from them and brought his army into winter quarters near Winchester.

Now in the winter camp, without the Yankees to engage their attention, they turned their mordant wit upon each other. Even Old Jack, in the fine new uniform which Beauty Stuart gave him, was not immune. "God Almighty!" shouted the soldiers, "Old Jack has drawed his bounty money and got hisse'f some clo'se."

It was indeed good in the Valley during those lingering autumnal days, when the blue haze intensified the color of the mountains and the sun still had a caressing heat, although the leaves burned red and gold. After all the marching and fighting, the soldiers found it good just to be alive, to sleep at night in the firm expectation of dawn, to rise confident of their rations with wild onions to prevent scurvy, and although they did not fatten on their meager flour and bacon, at least their stomachs were filled.

The happy respite could not last. The South had won the battles, but it had not won the war. On November 22, Jackson led his command over the familiar trail across the Blue Ridge to join Lee at Fredericksburg. This time the men knew well what to expect. They knew that they were going back to the dead-dog weariness of all-night marches, to the hungry waiting for wagons that were almost empty, to the hideous din of conflict, the fierce and always unexpected stare of death. They did not know where they were going, but Old Jack did. Their trust was in Old Jack.

From the top of the mountains they took a last look at their Valley, mistily lying below them, brown and green, threaded with a shining river. "It is a lovely Valley to fight for," their hearts said silently. "When shall we see it again?" Never, for one-quarter of the men, and for their leader, never.

An unspeakable sadness settled on the Valley when the troops had gone. The women wore black. Widows, mothers, sisters, sweethearts, scarcely a family was without a loss. The camps with their lack of sanitation had brought epidemics particularly hard upon the young and the very old. Almost everyone with little children saw at least one die. The women were tired. Those who had owned no slaves missed their men and struggled with the heavy chores. The others learned to bake, clean, and cook. They discovered the infinite patience needed for the care of little children when there were no warm black arms to hold them.

The Valley people could not hope to have the winter to themselves after the army went across the Blue Ridge. It was said that the citizens of Winchester did not know in the morning which side possessed them until they went downtown. General Milroy arrived on Jackson's heels and made a protracted visit. All through the winter the people groaned under him. A change had come in the temper of the conflict, "not the civil, but the *uncivil* war." The North was growing angry. The rebellion proved too hard to put down, the war was lasting too long.

It was food, the lack of food, that preoccupied everyone that winter. When General Milroy proclaimed that food would be sold only to those who took the Federal oath, some capitulated, but most preferred semistarvation.

*T*o all the brave young men who will not sing again under the Valley moonlight, to the lost riders, the lost marchers, the lost fighting men, add Jackson, the greatest fighter of them all. Stonewall Jackson, pressing on into the long darkness after Chancellorsville and the last river crossing. In the dark woods while gathering information, he was mistakenly shot by his own men.

He lost his left arm, but for a time it seemed he might survive. When pneumonia set in, Jackson said to his wife: "You are too frightened, my child. I think God still has work for me to do and will raise me up to do it." Later: "Doctor, Anna tells me I am to die today. Is that correct?" On confirmation, he lay a long time, silent, digesting and accepting the reality. At last he spoke. "Very good. It is all right." Jackson, the good soldier.

His body lay in state in Richmond, then was sent to Lexington. The VMI cadets escorted it. With the cortege went the sorrow-stricken hearts of the entire Confederacy. Jackson had said that he did not

Route 600, Frederick County

desire to outlive the independence of his country, that life was nothing without honor, that degradation was worse than death. Now for him and for two hundred thousand other Americans had come the silence, the unbreakable rest—but the living would have to struggle two years longer.

They buried General Jackson in his Valley at Lexington on May 15, 1863. His brigade could not have the privilege of escorting him to his last rest. Lee was in a new offensive and could not spare them for even a few days. They would never again see him slouch past on his uninspiring little horse, blushing at their cheers; never again would they hear the crisp voice at unexpected moments in the deadened weariness of a forced march, "Press on, men. Press on. Close up, men. Close up." They would never again see his flaming presence ride through the smoke of battle. "Steady, men, all's well. You must stand it an hour longer, men. You must hold out another hour." Never again would they have the same confidence in their ability to outflank and beat the Yankees. They felt his spirit with them as they fought, but they soon found that the spirit did not issue orders or plan strategy.

"You have lost your left arm," Lee wrote him when he was wounded, "but I have lost my right."

On June 14 the Confederates came back to Winchester, and Milroy left with flying coattails. The liberators were Jackson's old corps now fighting under Ewell, many in Jubal Early's division. After two days of rejoicing, the Army of Northern Virginia crossed the Potomac and marched on—to Gettysburg.

The people of the Valley did not know it but they had seen the high-water mark, the end of Confederate hopes and illusions, the end of life as they had known it. From then on, though the gray army was still to come back several times, the war in the Valley would be the Yankees' war.

The Burning

The Confederate army fell back through eastern Virginia, back to Brady Station, back to the bridge over the Rappahannock, back to winter quarters on the Rapidan, back to the Wilderness. As 1864 began, they had a new general opposing them, Ulysses S. Grant, in temper as dogged and indestructible as Stonewall Jackson, and backed by a numerical preponderance of two to one. If 140,000 men oppose 60,000, the larger number must inevitably win, Grant thought—and he was right.

The gray soldiers, with the instinct of old campaigners, sensed the difference, and some of the mirth went out of Lee's army. The stronger spirits were more determinedly sacrificial, and the fainter-hearted deserted more freely. In the spring of '64, Lee proclaimed that deserters would be pardoned if they came back within thirty days.

In the Valley two new stars were rising, and both wore blue. Where Ashby had ridden, now rode George Custer, and bluff Phil Sheridan was to be crowned with the ultimate success. Southern reminiscences grow reticent about this period, and the northerners take up the pen, for it is pleasanter to remember victory than defeat.

To the east, a new sort of soldier garrisoned Harpers Ferry—the 19th Regiment, black troops from Maryland. Their specific purpose was to recruit ex-slaves in the lower Valley.

A large number of black troops fought for the Union during the Civil War. Captain James J. Rickard of the 19th, a Rhode Islander who admired his men and wrote a memoir of his service with them, gives the total in the army as 186,097, of whom 36,847 died—numbers only slightly larger than those generally accepted by modern scholars. Neither Lincoln, Grant, nor Sherman at first favored their use as soldiers. They fought well at Petersburg and Richmond, and it was they who made the last charge at Appomattox.

National Cemetery, Winchester. Civil War dead from both sides lie buried here.

Now spring again brought the new green wheat thrusting through the freshly worked earth, brought the newborn lambs, brought the renewed necessity for killing. The Union general Franz Sigel fought a battle at New Market and was completely routed by a smaller force. The battle, on May 15, was neither large nor decisive. But New Market has a special claim upon the memory of the Valley, for it was there that the thinning southern ranks were strengthened by the cadets from VMI.

No reinforcements could be spared from the desperate defense of Richmond, so the lads closed their schoolbooks, stepped out in their light blue and scarlet, and marched into the guns as smartly as they had maneuvered on the drill grounds. During four years past, youths of seventeen or more had graduated from the institute as officers, until at this time many of the corps were barely adolescent. Some were so small that the women could lift them in their arms and carry them from the field.

On May 15 each year at Lexington, the VMI cadets assemble. The roll is called, and as each name is read, a first classman steps forward and replies: "Dead on the field of honor."

*A*ccording to the Federal reports, "The Shenandoah Valley was for us the Valley of humiliation." Halleck wired to Grant after New Market: "Sigel will do nothing but run. He never did anything else." Then General David Hunter was put in command of West Virginia. He was sixty-two, a West Pointer born of a Virginia family, son of a Presbyterian minister, and he fought against his relatives with all the fury of a convert.

The attack came soon, near Newtown eight miles south of Winchester, and Hunter sent the 1st New York Cavalry to burn "every house, store and outbuilding in that place except the churches. . . . You will also burn the houses of all the rebels between Newtown and Middletown."

When the detachment arrived in Newtown, women, children, and old men came out in tears. They were simple people, hard-working people. They proved that they had nursed Union soldiers who had been wounded, they proved that their young men were with Lee across the mountains and not with the notorious raider John Mosby.

Major Stearns listened carefully and listened also to his own men, who grumbled that "it was no part of a soldier's duty to burn the houses of noncombatants." In the end he decided to take the responsibility of disobedience, left the town intact, and reported all the circumstances to General Hunter, who let the matter drop.

At Lexington, however, the commanding general was on the scene in person, and the flames roared as he ordered. The Federal troops entered the town on Saturday, June 11. On Sunday, Hunter burned VMI, the houses of the professors, and the house of Governor Letcher. The statue of George Washington on the cupola of Washington College was taken down and shipped to Wheeling to save it from the "degenerate sons of worthy sires." Captain William McKinley and Colonel Rutherford B. Hayes helped people carry out their belongings.

As Hunter withdrew from Lexington, Early's men were on their way from eastern Virginia. They marched one hundred miles to Charlottesville in the old foot-cavalry style. Only three soldiers and the captain were left in Company A of the Stonewall Brigade. Of the original seventy-five, twenty-six had died, twenty-three had "gone home." The rest had been wounded or captured. Five generals had been killed while leading them. For a year they had fought on no more than a pint of cornmeal and a quarter pound of bacon daily. Still they had their bands, and as they marched through Staunton the bands were playing.

They were still fighting, they could hold or drive an enemy who outnumbered them three to one. Even the Federals found their courage "beyond all wonder and beyond all praise." What were they fighting for, these ragged, hungry, filthy men? Not for slaves, which four-fifths of them never hoped to have. Not for their civil government, for which they had little respect. Not because they clung to hopes of winning. They were fighting primarily for their leader. Ashby was dead, Jackson was dead, Stuart was dead, but Lee remained, and the army found no irreverence in bracketing him with God. They were fighting for "Old Marse," and they were fighting because they had forgotten how to quit.

These were the men who came back to the Valley, appalled at its devastation, who pursued Hunter to the west along a road lined with abandoned loot and smoking ruins, with women's dresses, broken china, children's toys trampled in the mud. Jackson's division filed past his unmarked grave in silence and dipped their tattered flags in homage. The Confederates swept another time down the Valley, routed the small force left to oppose them, reentered Winchester on July 2, and on the fifth crossed the Potomac into Maryland. They were only 14,000, with no hope of reinforcements and enemy armies all around them. On clear days they could see the white dome of the Capitol, gleaming like a mirage. They could also see the hastily summoned reinforcements filing into the breastworks. After two days, Early withdrew and brought his army back into the Valley, just ahead of the returning Hunter.

The temper of the war grew steadily grimmer. Hunter was in no conciliatory mood. Washington had not been pleased when he allowed Early to come so close to the city. On August 8, Hunter at his own request was relieved of his command, and another man took charge of crushing the resistance in the Valley.

His name was Philip Sheridan.

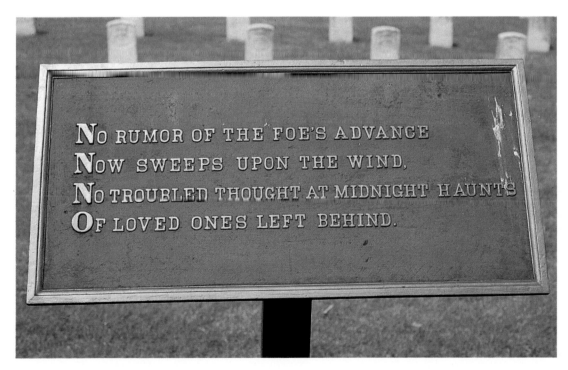

No RUMOR OF THE FOE'S ADVANCE
Now SWEEPS UPON THE WIND,
No TROUBLED THOUGHT AT MIDNIGHT HAUNTS
OF LOVED ONES LEFT BEHIND.

*National Cemetery,
Winchester*

Up from the South, at break of day,
Bringing to Winchester fresh dismay,
The affrighted air with a shudder bore,
Like a herald in haste, to the chieftain's door,
The terrible grumble, and rumble and roar,
Telling the battle was on once more,
And Sheridan twenty miles away.
—Thomas Buchanan Read, "Sheridan's Ride"

CHAPTER 20

The Starving Crows

General Sheridan's army, 35,000 strong at Harpers Ferry, was named the Army of the Shenandoah, a fact that gave small satisfaction to the inhabitants of the Valley. The hearty new commander, a West Pointer with a bluff and humorous face, born of Irish parents at Albany, roused the loyalty and admiration of his troops in a way that his predecessors had not. He had fought Indians, he had done fine work with his cavalry in the west. Now he had an army of his own.

Grant had recognized clearly that attrition was his infallible weapon. When he lost 60,000 men in campaigning from the Wilderness to Petersburg, whereas Lee opposed him with no more than 68,000, he did not falter. His plan was as subtle as a bludgeon: "eat out Virginia clear and clean . . . so that crows flying over it . . . will have to carry their provender with them. . . . If the war is to last another year, we want the Shenandoah Valley to remain a barren waste."

Sheridan was the right man to carry out such orders.

As the Union reinforcements poured into the Valley, the Confederates watched them from their signal post on top of Massanutten. During the first two weeks of September, the cavalry fought almost daily—"Handsome dashes," Sheridan called them. He quartered at Rion Hall, near Charles Town. On September 15, Grant visited him there, for the weary Mr. Lincoln had told him that "there will be nothing done unless you watch it every day and hour, and force it." But after one talk Grant felt satisfied that Sheridan would need no order save "Go in."

The armies feinted, advanced, withdrew, and advanced again. Early's thin cavalrymen were never at rest two days in succession. The Valley people called the Pike the "soldiers' racetrack," called the blue Army of the Shenandoah "Harpers Weekly" because it showed up at the Ferry every week. By mid-September, Sheridan had 56,764 men against Early's 12,509.

Sheridan pressed on to Harrisonburg, then on to Staunton with his cavalry everywhere carrying out their work of destruction. Every barn, every mill, each haystack, they burnt; every cow, every steer, every horse, pig, sheep, or hen, they slaughtered or drove off.

The first large battle of the last campaign was fought just east of Winchester on September 19. The Federal divisions came up slowly, and two of the subordinate Union generals considered that they had saved the day on their own initiative. Nevertheless, Sheridan had the proper presence and spirit that the men had been waiting for. "We sent them whirling through Winchester and we are after them tomorrow," he reported. The Confederates dug in at Fisher's Hill, were routed, and fled up the Pike through Narrow Passage and back to the old camp at Brown's Gap.

At the end of September, Sheridan decided that his supply lines were too extended and withdrew back down the Valley, burning as he went. He scorched the countryside, making it a barren waste. The crows would need their provender in flying over, but the people of the Valley could not fly. They were offered free transportation north with the receding Army of the Shenandoah. Only the oldest or the most fainthearted availed themselves of the opportunity. The rest stayed on their land to face down starvation.

Sheridan reported that he had burned 2,000 barns, 120 flour mills, destroyed or carried away 874 barrels of flour, 22,000 bushels of oats, 460,072 bushels of wheat, 51,380 tons of hay, 157,076 bushels of corn. He drove off 16,438 head of cattle, 16,141 hogs, 17,837 sheep, took 10,000 pounds of tobacco, 2,500 bushels of potatoes, tore up 947 miles of railroad, and the houses were not spared. The damage was estimated at $25 million. The destruction included the Luray and Fort Valleys as well as the main Valley. Well satisfied with his achievement, Sheridan moved his army to a strong position north of Fisher's Hill and made a hasty trip to Washington, where Congress passed a vote of confidence in him and his men.

As Sheridan withdrew, Rosser's Laurel Brigade (once Ashby's) came through Brown's Gap to reinforce Early. Looking down from the mountain they could see a cloud of smoke across the Valley from the Blue Ridge to North Mountain. The smoke rolled up from the rich fields. By night the sky glared red and the earth was starred with bonfires. Most of the command were Valley men, who now watched their own homes and farms burning. Where they could avenge, they gave no quarter.

Rosser's men found themselves twenty-five miles ahead of Early, with the Federals between them.

On the morning of October 19, Early attacked Sheridan's army just above Cedar Creek by marching past a Union left flank resting on the North Fork of the Shenandoah where it curves around the spurred foot of Signal Knob. The attack began at four-thirty in the predawn, and a light fog added to the confusion. The surprise was complete; the Rebels passed the pickets and took the breastworks in five minutes. The sleepy 19th, USA, breakfasting in the darkness, heard the Rebel yell. As the fog lifted they saw the whole gray army in front of them. They held gallantly until bullets flew into them from the rear. Their general sent an aide in haste "to tell the First Division to stop firing." But the aide came back more quickly than he went, for the men at the rear were Rosser's Rebels.

Within an hour the whole Federal army was pouring down the Pike in disorder with the Rebels after them, but not as hotly as Early wished, for the hungry southerners gave way to their fatal propensity for plundering.

Meanwhile in Winchester, some fifteen miles from Cedar Creek, at 6 A.M., a courier brought news of the battle to General Sheridan, who had stopped there for the night on his way back from Washington. Sheridan was at first inclined to think the morning action was just a skirmish. He breakfasted comfortably and mounted between eight and nine. He had not covered more than three or four miles when he began to meet the flying troops, then the wagons, with the drivers lashing sweating teams, then the hurrying confusion of the main army. He ordered a stop to the flight, put spurs to his black charger, and flew up the Pike.

"Face about, boys, and follow me. We will lick the whole damn Rebel army!"

The men cheered and turned back, and as the general galloped on, cheers rolled up from the Pike from regiment to regiment, division to division, and the army took fresh heart.

After a spirited gallop of about five miles, Sheridan reorganized his army at Newtown and ordered them to charge and take back the position they had just vacated, riding himself along the re-formed lines, encouraging them in his earnest animated way: "Boys, if I had been here, this never would have happened. Now we are going back to our camps. We are going to get a twist on them. We are going to lick them out of their boots."

He breathed his spirit into his men, and they responded nobly, counterattacking and breaking the Rebel charge. After fighting all day in the hot sun without food or water, evening found the Yankees

Blue Ridge Mountains near Compton, Route 340, Page County

back in their old camp, where they flung themselves down and slept among the dead. The cavalry pursued the flying Confederates as far as Woodstock.

So the last thrust had been tried and had failed. Sheridan took his army back to Winchester, where he was made a major general. Early camped for two months near New Market, then withdrew to winter quarters at Staunton.

That was the starving winter. In the homes up and down the Valley, beside the blackened embers of the barns, the women found that life could be sustained all day on a roll and a cup of chickory coffee, that milk and mush made a royal supper for the children after beans and sorghum molasses.

The cavalry was still active. In October, Mosby's men made their "Greenback Raid" on a train near Harpers Ferry and captured $75,000 in gold from two Federal paymasters. General Sheridan wrote to Halleck, "I will soon commence work on Mosby."

When the frost had killed the grass and the cold rains started, it looked as though Rosser's cavalry might have to disband for the lack of forage. The troopers could tighten their belts and live on a handful of flour, but they could not stand it when their horses began to die in camp of starvation. So that they might be fed, Early let a quarter of his command go home on leave as soon as the roads became impassable for armies.

But it was all unavailing, all the endurance, all the gallantry, all the unbelievable determination in the face of hardships. They could not win. They were fighting against time, against the greater dream. But let America take due pride in their courage, for they were her sons.

At the end of February, Sheridan moved again, attacked Early at Waynesboro, flanked him, and destroyed the remainder of his command. The Federals took eleven hundred prisoners, and Early barely escaped through the underbrush. Rosser made a flying attack on the Federal column to allow the prisoners to escape, but they did not want to escape. They had had enough.

So ended the movement of large armies in the Valley. On March 6, Sheridan crossed the Shenandoah and departed by the way of the James River Canal, which he destroyed.

Now only Mosby's troopers hung on, without a camp or headquarters, raiding when they could and returning after each sally to the shelter of the Blue Ridge, "that beautiful blue mountain," which was their safety and their home. Desertions increased, for the men drifted back to their starving families.

The spring brought Appomattox, where on April 9 General Lee surrendered the last eight thousand of what had been his army.

It was over. Americans no longer had to kill each other. Out of an army of two and a half million the Union had lost nearly four hundred thousand. Out of a million the South had lost nearly two hundred thousand.

It was over, and the beautiful Valley lay a barren waste. The weary soldiers limped home to blasted trees and blackened fields, stark chimneys rising out of crumbling walls, eyeless windows, silence and devestation. All that men could do to ruin the Valley had been done—but the land remained, the limestone and the river, the courage and the hope in human hearts, as frail and persistent as grass.

"Let your men keep their horses, general," said Grant to Lee. "They will need them for spring plowing."

Furl that banner, for tis weary;
Round its staff it's drooping dreary.
Furl it, fold it,—it is best.
For there's not a man to wave it,
And there's not a sword to save it,
And there's not one left to lave it
In the blood which heroes gave it,
And its foes now scorn and brave it.
    Furl it, hide it,—let it rest.
       —Father Ryan, "The Conquered Banner"

CHAPTER 21

The Hero

One afternoon in early autumn of 1865, a solitary traveler, wearing a gray military coat from which the buttons and insignia had been removed, rode into Lexington on an iron-gray horse. Although his arrival was as unostentatious as possible, a few passersby recognized him and turned to follow him quietly. So with the utmost simplicity General Robert E. Lee began his tenure as president of Washington College.

He had not come because of a tempting offer, for the fortunes of the little college had never been at so low an ebb. He had come to discharge a responsibility his conscience laid upon him.

All through the Valley that summer, all through Virginia, all through the Confederacy, the boys were coming home—riding their broken-down horses, tramping down dusty lanes—returning not to efficient hospitalization, mustering-out pay, a bonus from a grateful government, but to silence, poverty, labor, bitterness, defeat. These were the young men who had left their youth behind them on the blood-stained fields, who had learned nothing since boyhood save to kill and to survive. Half their brothers slept beneath the wheat, but the homecomers could not sleep. They had to find what they could do in their ruined land, what aptitudes they had for which society would pay them with bread. They had to train their minds and school their hearts—but most of all, they must learn to forget, to forget the terror

and the glory, the lost vain hopes, and to forget the bitterness. They had followed Lee bravely, giving all the bright young morning of their lives. Now he would dedicate his evening to their service.

The general was a defeated warrior, a paroled prisoner of war, excluded from the general amnesty. Many voices in the North were calling for his blood, insisting that he ought to be hanged. The radical party in Congress might have succeeded in having him tried for treason had not General Grant threatened to resign his commission if the terms of the surrender were violated. Of his personal fortune nothing remained. His house and lands were confiscated, his career as a professional soldier was closed. He retained nothing except the unanimous love and veneration of the people in the South.

He lived quietly that first summer with his invalid wife and two daughters in a four-room cottage on a friend's place near Richmond, and ignored the threats that constantly appeared against him in the northern press. He refused a country home in England and a hacienda in Mexico. He also refused all commercial offers. His reputation was not for sale, and what remained of his life belonged to his country, to that impoverished Virginia with which his fortunes were irrevocably involved. He declined the presi-

Edward Valentine's sculpture of Robert E. Lee in repose. Lee Chapel, Washington and Lee University, Lexington. Lee and his family lie in a crypt below the memorial.

Two does, Skyline Drive

dency of Sewanee in Tennessee because it was a denominational college, and of the University of Virginia since it was a state institution. When the offer came from Washington College, he hesitated—not because it was struggling, depleted, and comparatively unknown, but because he was "an object of censure to a portion of the country, and my connection might be injurious to it."

The board of trustees overrode his objections. When he accepted, they could hardly believe their good fortune. Individually and collectively, they were in a state of absolute poverty. The faculty was reduced to three, the students to not more than fifty. Most of the equipment had been destroyed by General Hunter. Judge Brockenbrough had to borrow a suit before he could go to Richmond and make the offer. They promised Lee a salary of $1,500 a year and a house, but they felt obligated to explain that the college was $4,000 in debt and that they counted on an increased enrollment under his presidency to pay their bills. It was a beginning, and so Lee understood it.

He put the past behind him and marched forward with a calm serenity. "Misfortune nobly borne is good fortune," he quoted to the sculptor Edward V. Valentine. Only once did someone see his composure broken. He left the chapel one morning with a look of extreme distress, and a lady with more concern than tact asked him what could be the matter.

"I was thinking, madam, of my responsibility to God for all of these young men."

General Lee's broken-down college had a long history. The Scotch-Irish, as concerned about education as they were about religion, founded in 1749 a "classical academy" at Timber Ridge, where Latin, Greek, algebra, and geometry were taught in a one-room log cabin. In 1776, in the spirit of the times, the school's name was changed from Augusta Academy to Liberty Hall. In 1796, George Washington made Liberty Hall—relocated to Lexington—a present of his shares in the James River Canal and permitted the name to be changed to Washington College. For about fifty years the school proceeded quietly on its way while students came and went, to the accompaniment of complaints about the lack of respect accorded their elders. Then the Liberty Hall Volunteers marched off in the spring of 1861.

When General Lee took over the ruin that four years of war had made, he knew that the South's greatest need was for education, and his ideas on the subject were clear-cut and consistent. "We have but one rule here," he said, "and it is that every student must be a gentleman." It was not an invitation to laxity. Lee tried to know all his students personally, even when he had eight hundred of them. He talked in warm and fatherly terms with any who offended by misconduct or idleness. But if reformation did not follow, the young man was dropped.

Because they had fought in the Confederate army, the fathers of youths at Lexington were disfranchised, and so were many of the students. Virginia was neither in the Union nor out of it. She had become Military District One. She had not been allowed to secede, and now she might not be represented in the national Congress. Even her state officials were held incompetent to serve because of their connection with the rebellion.

Amid the dark postwar currents of hatred, fury and revenge; amid ruin, lawlessness, and pillage; amid defeat and confusion, apathy and despair—General Lee at Lexington stood like a beacon by which to steer. If he felt regret or sadness, he did not utter it; if he noticed a difference in his circumstances, he did not refer to it; if he felt critical of the new authorities, he did not say so. To all the parents who sent their sons to his institution, he gave the same advice: "Remember that we form one country now. Abandon all local animosities and make your sons Americans."

For five years Lee guided, built, encouraged, and led—then death came for him, not stealthily or suddenly, but as a last antagonist whom an old soldier might calmly face. One evening as he stood to say grace before tea, he found himself unable to speak and sank back in his chair. Afterward, he lay quietly in bed for two weeks, perfectly conscious and apparently in no pain, rarely speaking, never complaining, but "neither expecting nor desiring to get well." In his last hours his mind wandered slightly. "Strike the tent," he said. "Tell Hill he must come up."

They laid him in the crypt of the new chapel. Today above his remains rests the recumbent statue that Valentine carved out of white marble.

Even then the people of America knew that he belonged to all of them, not only to the South. Julia Ward Howe wrote a commemorative poem for him, Charles Francis Adams and Gamaliel Bradford paid him tribute.

It is a good thing for Americans, with their worship of success, to have one hero who was magnificent in failure.

CHAPTER 22

Fool's Gold and True Gold

During the last thirty years of the nineteenth century the people of the Valley were concerned with one absorbing problem—the necessity of making a living. Yet somehow, in 1890, they found themselves squarely in the middle of a land boom. No new discoveries of natural resources had been made, the climate remained in winter cold and in summer hot, but overnight, by a kind of mass hysteria, Valley land seemed to have become immensely valuable. The promoters came with brassy voices and bright promises, and culled their harvest from the gullible. Every Valley town grabbed for its slice of pie. They built Basic City, Buena Vista, Glasgow. At Goshen, Jim Aldred invested in a lot but was frightened away by meeting a bear on the supposed main street of the imagined city. Along the curving reaches of the river, beside the springs, and in even more unlikely places, rose huge rambling hotels crowned with wooden gables, cupolas, and fretwork. Then it was over. As mysteriously as it had begun, the vision faded. Many were disappointed and some were poorer.

But the Valley was to have a source of revenue more solid than the paper real estate—a tangible, fragrant, succulent basis of income. The earliest settlers had discovered that apples would thrive in the Valley; among other things, these worthies used the fruit for making brandy. Queen Victoria gave an

impetus to Virginia apple growing because she so relished a barrel given her that she removed the tariff on their importation. Even so, apples were not grown on a large scale until the bustling 1890s.

Miss Lizzie and Miss Julia Terrill were saving their money to go to the Philadelphia Centennial of 1876, when an apple tree salesman arrived at their door. They never got to the centennial; instead, they put in one of the first big orchards in the Valley.

It is to be hoped that the Misses Terrill were in no hurry for a return on their investment. Apple growing is for the patient and laborious. The farmer must plant yearling shoots and wait from seven to twelve years before they bear fruit. There are the spring frosts to destroy the blossoms; the summer droughts to dwarf the apples; the coddling moth; the scab; the scale; in a good year, a labor shortage that makes picking impossible, or an overproduction that gluts the market and sends prices below profit. Yet in spite of foreboding, anxiety, and moments of depression, the fruit does ripen. By autumn the trees are

Rinker's Apple Orchard, west of Stephens City, Frederick County

Insecticide spraying, Rinker's Apple Orchard

In August, the apples are ready for picking in the lower Valley

Miguel Morez, migrant
worker, on the job at apple-
picking time

jeweled with red and yellow, the branches sagging in the mellow light, the countryside enveloped in rich fragrance.

The hardest labor is ahead, for now the fruit must be picked, packed, and marketed. Into the Valley pours a flood of itinerant laborers, thousands of them, as migratory as locusts, settling over the landscape for a brief two months. The picking is a grueling season. The farmer must rise before dawn and work after dark with the last reserve of strength, for nature moves on relentlessly, fruit falls to rot as soon as it has ripened.

At the packing plants the round and shining apples are poured onto conveyor belts, pass over a sorting mesh, roll into an acid bath that washes off the sprays, and are waxed to leave them gleaming.

At last it is over. The freight cars roll away heavily laden, the applesauce and cider factories have their quota, the greater portion of the crop has gone into cold-storage plants, to be released as demand occurs.

Apples ready for processing into applesauce or juice, Bowman's Apple Products, Mount Jackson, Shenandoah County

Mary Carter and Ruth Ann Lear sorting apples by grade before shipment, Hearty Apple Packing, Meems, Shenandoah County

The dry leaves fall, and winter quietly settles on the orchards. Under the cold moon, gnarled trees sleep with their crooked branches baldly exposed. There is no one now to walk between and tend them, only little round-eared mice gnawing at the roots.

Then the long-expected and unhurried spring arrives. The rolling earth stretches itself, and overnight the gray trees throw a veil of blossoms across the ridge and hollow. The farmer looks at the orchard, fairer than a garden, and feels that to be an apple grower is a blessed thing.

Past into the Present

*T*ime passed into another century. The Civil War became just a story for the old ones. The aging soldiers, fewer every year, had known the ultimate in danger, comradeship, despair, and happiness. Now even Mosby, despite his patch over one eye and his dashing hat, was an old man who talked gallantly to the ladies at the horse show. Of the war nothing remained save the young look in grandfather's eyes while he played "Dixie" for the children on a paper-covered comb.

The women talked more than the men about the past. They had hoped until hope turned to bitterness; they had worked until work gnarled their hands and bowed their shoulders; they had gone without and made a virtue of their necessities. They reared their children and preserved their gracious manners. It was vulgar to be rich, they said. Nice people never had any money.

The tempo of life moved slowly in the Valley, old houses slipped further into decay, old brick sidewalks became a little more uneven. Cool the houses were in those days, with a scrubbed smell, dark, always with some rooms little aired, where old mahogany furniture, family portraits hung crookedly on the walls, hair wreathes and peacock-feather fans, glass bells over dried flowers, all conspired to embalm the past.

Home of Charles and
Barbara Hunter, Route 250,
West Augusta, Augusta
County

Chicken barbecue,
Bluegrass Festival, Skyline
Drive

On Valley farms, owners worked in muddy boots and sweat-stained shirts. Somehow each year, with strong hands the wheat was garnered, corn husked or chopped for silage, sheep sheared, hogs butchered, hay mowed. Gaiety had not vanished. To give a dance meant only to move the furniture aside, bake a cake and make some lemonade and turn on the victrola. There would be well-chaperoned camps on the Shenandoah with canoes, campfires, and singing. The young people enjoyed themselves.

Slowly, the mud-stained buggies and tired horses that once lined both sides of Main Street gave way to equally mud-stained automobiles. The roads had not yet improved in relation to the new rapid transportation. Still in spring the deep ruts twisted axles; in summer the thick dust flew like a smoke barrage and smothered those behind. They soon macadamized the lower Pike, but in some upper sections

Charles Clements using velocipede saw, Museum of American Frontier Culture

Glazed-brick silo, Route 664 near Sherando, Augusta County

Powell's Fort in Fort Valley, Route 771, Shenandoah County

the old plank road of rotting logs remained into the second decade of the twentieth century. Not until 1918 were the tolls abolished that had made it cost $4.75 to drive from Winchester to Staunton.

A Charles Town man in 1896 took a great step toward ending rural isolation, when Postmaster General William L. Wilson established the first rural free delivery route in the United States. The carriers were to cover twenty miles a day on horseback. It was not until one of them complained of having to open and shut sixty-three gates on his route that the farmers were asked to place mailboxes along the road.

Peace dwelt in the blue air cupped between the mountain ranges, in the shaded towns surrounded by the fields. Prosperity also, if the measure of prosperity be that a family can live pleasantly in agreeable surroundings, maintained by work they find not too difficult. If no one grew rich in the Valley, no one starved.

In 1912 a man born in the Shenandoah Valley was elected president of the United States. Woodrow Wilson arrived in this world on December 28, 1856, at the Presbyterian manse in Staunton, where his

Byrd's Rest 3 on the Appalachian Trail, milepost 34, Skyline Drive. The 2,000-mile trail from Maine to Georgia follows the crest of the Blue Ridge through Virginia.

Woodrow Wilson Museum, Staunton. The future president was born in a townhouse adjacent to this site in 1856.

Route 654, Highland County

Owen and Gary Breeden
at their sawmill, Jollett, Page
County. Small local sawmills
still provide lumber for many
Valley builders.

Shenandoah Mountain
viewed from the west near
Doe Hill, Route 624, Highland
County

Route 619, Highland County   father was the minister. The historic event occasioned no excitement at the time and the family moved on before Woodrow was three. But Staunton claims him and has turned his birthplace into a shrine.

Across the world the winds of war were piling up another tidal wave, and again the peaceful Valley was swept into the storm. This time her sons were taken far away. They went willingly. In one county, out of the 565 called for examination, only 5 claimed any exemption. Many volunteered before the draft board reached them. The streets were brave with flags. For the first time in fifty years the Stars and Stripes floated above the doorways. But at doorway after doorway it was flown with the Stars and Bars.

This was natural, for in the Valley they know that the past and the present are coexistent in time, and that no one walks into the future without both of them.

Valley Tour I

The present and past have flowed together. A road rides the crest of the old Blue Ridge. The Skyline Drive, born out of the depression, undulates for 107 miles along the summit of the Ridge—over the lava, the basalt, granite, the inestimably ancient rocks where Lederer and Spotswood painfully climbed. The traveler can see the panorama of the Valley from the points where the European explorers, and before them, the Iroquois and the Catawba, saw it, and like them can behold that it is fair.

From Hazeltop, Skyland, and Stony Man, from Old Rag Mountain, Hawksbill, Big Meadows, Thornton Hollow, and Hogback, it is all there—the checkered rolling fields, the toy-house towns, the occasional chimney with a gray plume, the frowning bulk of Massanutten making the Luray Valley dear and close, and the Shenandoah twisting grandly through the fertile land.

The wooded mountains around the Skyline Drive have been made into the Shenandoah National Park, to belong forever to the people of the United States. In 1924 Hubert Work, secretary of the interior, appointed a commission to find a park site in the east. They were persuaded to come to Skyland, a camping resort near Stony Man Mountain. After they left they voted unanimously for the Blue Ridge.

The government did not buy the land but merely promised to improve it after it had been donated. In a truly American spirit of voluntary cooperation, the citizens of Virginia raised a million dollars by

Tunnel through St.
Mary's Rock, near milepost
32, Skyline Drive

Amy Deller (left) weighs
bear cub near Gooney Run
Overlook, milepost 7, Skyline
Drive. Scientists regularly
monitor black bear population
and habitat in Shenandoah
National Park.

Visitors to Skyland ride the
trail to Limberlost, a scenic
forest of tall pines and cedars,
near milepost 43, Skyline
Drive.

*Work on stone wall, part
of a major renovation project
on the Skyline Drive*

Fall foliage, Skyline Drive

James Cook keeps alive the basket-weaving skills of the early settlers, Skyline Drive

South Fork at Bentonville, Warren County

donation to buy the mountains from the mountaineers. The state legislature added another million, 183,311 acres were set aside, and the drive was built. President Franklin Roosevelt conducted the ceremony of dedication of the Shenandoah National Park in 1936 at Big Meadows.

Willingly or unwillingly, the mountaineers sold their homes—the crooked cabins, the clearings, the steep patches where, they say, a farmer has to hang onto a root with one hand while he hoes with the other, and has to plant corn by shooting the seed into the hill. True mountain stock, isolationists par excellence, they had preserved their dialect, their old ballads, their dulcimers, their weaving, and their fierce independence. Some moved when they sold their homes, others stayed on by a lifetime agreement with the government, but the old ways were broken.

The mountain world calls to peace. It is a high, clear, untroubled world where the complications of life seem to drop away. In the first year after its opening, the Shenandoah National Park had 776,880 visitors. It is the city people now who love the narrow trails that meander secretly through the flower-jeweled woods beside sparkling brooks, and who like to lie in the sun on high rocks and watch the buzzards hanging in the air below them, and the Valley spread out like a rich carpet.

For the botanist or ornithologist, the Park is a paradise. Every sort of plant flourishes in the moderate climate, and migratory birds stop on their annual journeys. Eighty varieties of trees grow on the slopes. The wildflower families number more than a thousand. Spring brings the redbud, azalea, and the dogwood like puffs of pink and white smoke along the hills, and summer the pink rose and glossy green of rhododendron and mountain laurel. In the damp ferny hollows hide small, shy flowers, hepatica and bloodroot, orchids, anemones, wintergreen, ladies tresses and some rare plants not found elsewhere outside the Arctic Circle.

Passage Creek in flood, 1992. Spring storms turned the normally tranquil creek in Fort Valley into a raging torrent.

Bobby Beahm performing at Bluegrass Festival, Skyline Drive. Bluegrass music is a Valley favorite.

Bridge leading into Front Royal over the South Fork, Route 340

Front Royal in spring

Memorial Day, Warren County Courthouse, Front Royal

Randolph-Macon Academy, Front Royal

Near Browntown,
Warren County

Poor House Farm, near Browntown, is a landmark visible from the Skyline Drive.

Most of this the tourists miss. They spin along and stop in keen enjoyment, for here on the heights above the Shenandoah they grasp, for a moment, the illusion of something that has never existed save as a hope still glimmering in the human mind—the illusion of perfect freedom.

Roll down to Front Royal, down into the Valley from the Blue Ridge—not hurrying through, but slowly and quietly, taking time to discover her secrets. The face of the Valley is best revealed along the narrow curving backroads that wind between honeysuckle-covered banks and wander along the reaches of the Shenandoah, under the willows and the sycamores. Lost, quiet little roads that cross the river casually on low-water bridges only a foot or two above the swirling eddies. This is the Valley of the Shenandoah, a deep sweet land, where the evenings are full of loveliness, the morning fresh with the dew from heaven.

Valley Tour II

Fourteen miles down the Page Valley from Front Royal lies Luray, another town that has stepped cheerfully into the present, for there are "The Beautiful Caverns, Miles of Subterranean Splendor, Brilliantly Lighted by Electricity, a Playground of Giants, A Garden of Fairies, The World's Most Unusual Organ!"

There is a road out of Luray that climbs across the rugged crest of Massanutten, with trees pressing in on either side and the air growing perceptibly thinner and purer upon ascent. On the top of the mountain a narrow footpath, smelling of the damp green forest, leads to overlooks. To the west is revealed that hidden vale within the mountain, Fort Valley. Farther on, another overlook reveals the magnificent Page Valley.

Fort Valley is a golden retreat where clean toy houses and toy fields are enclosed forever from the world, enfolded in perpetual serenity and security. There an Englishman named Powell once stamped out his counterfeit money, which is said to have assayed a higher content of silver than the legitimate coin of the era; and there General Washington planned to make his last stand in event of failure. It would be best, perhaps, never to descend into Fort Valley, but to let the imagination possess it as the epitome of safety and peace.

Entrance building, Luray Caverns. Acidic groundwater leaching through limestone created numerous caverns in the Valley, many of them open to visitors.

Joan Niemeyer in Luray Caverns. Among the caverns' unusual features is a stone organ using natural calcium deposits to sound musical tones.

The highway south from Luray hugs the mountains, skips over the winding Green River on short bridges, sails through a little town where once was a popular resort, Bear Lithia Springs, past where Adam Miller settled; passes through Elkton, where once there was an ironworks; passes near a house where once Gabriel Jones, king's attorney, practiced; crosses the Spotswood Trail, from which a royal governor once viewed the Valley; comes to Port Republic, where was once was fought a battle and where another cavern exists.

Twenty miles below the frowning southern end of Massanutten, the town of Waynesboro has become an industrial center. On the mountaintop above near Rockfish Gap, is the site of Leakes Tavern, where on a summer day in 1818 some twenty-eight gentlemen of Virginia, among them Jefferson, Madison, Marshall, and Monroe, met to select the site for a new state university, and chose Charlottesville. Today the mountaintop is ornamented by a white marble mansion, Swannanoa, built in the style of the Italian Renaissance by Major Dooley of Richmond.

In the Valley, they have seen the dreamers and enterprises come and go. One thing they have learned. In the marrow of their bones, where it is inaccessible to reason and despair, they know that a dream matters more than its achievement. We do not always realize our aspirations, but the important thing is to build a new hope on the ruins of an old one, to go forward, to fight on.

Thirty miles from Waynesboro lies Lexington, where Lee rests in his chapel, and Jackson under his monument in the green cemetery on the hill. Valentine modeled Lee recumbent in white marble, Jackson standing in bronze. It was long after the battles before the South could gather money for Jackson's monument. When they at last erected it, the surviving Confederate soldiers came for a reunion. The

*Storybook wedding.
Diane and Wayne Stephens
are married by the Reverend
Wayne Bryant on Storybook
Trail, at the summit of
Massanutten Mountain.*

*Fort Valley viewed from
trail near Route 675, west of
Luray. At points along the trail,
hikers can look down into Fort
Valley on one side and across
Page Valley to the Blue Ridge
on the other.*

elderly remnants of the Stonewall Brigade chose to sleep in the open among the graves, holding a last bivouac with their general.

Dry Run United Church of Christ, Fort Valley

Lexington does not lack memorials. Moses Ezekiel, once a cadet who charged at New Market, made the bronze statue of Virginia mourning for her children that stands before his institute, VMI. George Washington's effigy has been returned, to crown again the cupola of his university. Cyrus McCormick stands on the campus by virtue of an endowment.

One road from Lexington leads to Goshen Pass, a lovely gorge with renowned waters. The way lies past the ghost of Rockbridge Springs, a resort whose glory has departed, and crosses the Alleghenies to "the Warm" and "the Hot Springs." The Homestead now keeps residence there. In another direction from Lexington, on the way to Roanoke, is the Natural Bridge, an unhewn stone arch over Cedar Creek. Thomas Jefferson was so impressed with it that he bought it from King George for twenty shillings, built a log cabin there, and installed a guest book. Young George Washington climbed it and carved his initials in the rock.

Route 678, Fort Valley

Charolais cattle, Fort Valley

Camp Roosevelt, Route 675, Page County. During the Great Depression, this Civilian Conservation Corps camp housed workers building the Skyline Drive and Shenandoah National Park.

*Marine Corps captains from
the Officers Training School at
Quantico, Virginia, study
tactics in a field exercise
atop Massanutten Mountain.*

*L. L. Huffman home,
Route 616, Alma,
Page County*

On the way back to Lexington stand two "boom" towns of the 1890s: Buena Vista, still active and industrial; and Glasgow, where a company headed by General Fitzhugh Lee built a hotel and a power-house, neither of which has ever operated. Glasgow is worthy of notice for the homes Green Forest and Glasgow Manor, built in the late eighteenth century by the great-grandfather of the novelist Ellen Glasgow.

Route 340 south of Shenandoah, Page County

The Shenandoah Valley has a proud connection with modern American literature, for it has Ellen Glasgow anchored at one end by her ancestral roots, and Willa Cather born at the other. The old brick Cather house sits in a hollow below the road between Romney and Winchester.

Staunton, a town of steep, hilly streets, looks to the grave of its founder, John Lewis, two miles outside of town. It is the birthplace of Woodrow Wilson and the home of Mary Baldwin College and the Staunton Military Academy. To the east lies the state-run Museum of American Frontier Culture, depicting early Valley life. Staunton invented the city manager form of government, in 1908.

From Staunton to Harrisonburg, the Valley is broad and smiling—immaculate Mennonite farms pattern the landscape where once Indians terrorized Augusta County by swooping down from North

Mountain. Here Daniel Boone married Rebecca Bryan. The Natural Chimneys, in a lovely park, provide the setting for the National Jousting Tournament. The Old Stone Church that John Craig led still stands square and solid. The road west leads over Shenandoah Mountain, the scene of the battle, and on to Monterey in the Virginia highlands, where now a maple sugar festival is held each spring.

Harrisonburg has a new look, a square-set neatness not always found in Valley towns. Here are no jagged corners of old stone, no flaking weather-beaten paint, no sagging walls. The buildings of James Madison University and the courthouse are massive and orderly, the streets fresh and clean. Eastern

Rusted relic of a bygone era: Model A Ford, Route 644 near Massanutten Resort, Rockingham County

Cattle-loading chute
near Alma, Page County

Vergile Cunningham at his
and his wife Bettie's Mountaintop Ranch, Jollett, Page
County

Porch, Mountaintop Ranch

Tony Lowe, farrier, shoeing
quarter horse at Mountaintop
Ranch

Milkweed pod in fall, Augusta County

Fountain at Swannanoa, a white marble mansion built by a Major Dooley of Richmond on the crest of the Blue Ridge at Rockfish Gap, near Waynesboro

The Colonnade at Washington and Lee University, Lexington

Mt. Pleasant at Buffalo Forge, Route 608, Rockbridge County

Norfolk & Western worker repairing track near Elkton, Rockingham County

Virginia Horse Center, Rockbridge County north of Lexington

Mennonite College represents the large community surrounding the town. The fields of Rockingham County are lush and wide, and by the side of one of them stands a marker: "Ashby fell here."

    In the Shenandoah Valley the present cannot be separated from the past for each contains the other, and the future is their child. The Valley Pike—the Long Gray Trail—runs north from Harrisonburg, and if the ghosts of long-dead soldiers ever walk, some will be marching here.

Sherando Lake,
Augusta County

*Homestead Inn, Hot Springs,
Bath County*

*Natural Bridge, a 214-foot
limestone arch over Cedar
Creek once owned by Thomas
Jefferson and now a popular
tourist attraction, Rockbridge
County*

Steel truss bridge over Buffalo
Creek, Route 251 near Murat,
Rockbridge County

Pat Buckley Moss
Museum, west of Waynesboro

Tom Martin at the Farmers'
Market, Roanoke

*Mary Baldwin College,
Staunton*

*A bronze turkey at the
Rockingham County line
on Route 11 announces the
county's main industry.*

Oak Grove Church, Dayton.
Among the earliest settlers of
the Valley, Mennonites form
a substantial part of the
population.

Staunton's "Jumbo," a
1911 Robinson pumper fire
truck—the last of its kind

Rockingham County Courthouse,
Harrisonburg

Old Order Mennonites, Rock
ingham County.

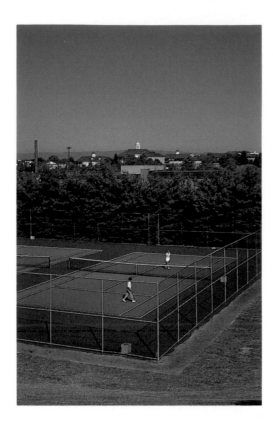

James Madison University,
Harrisonburg

Turkey farm,
Route 42 near Harrisonburg

Roger Lee's Buckhorn
Inn, Route 250 near West
Augusta, Augusta County. The
inn once hosted Stonewall
Jackson and his wife.

Route 613,
Rockingham County

Route 250 west of Monterey,
Highland County

Trout farming, a growing
industry in the Valley, Route
220 south of Monterey

Route 624 near Doe
Hill, Highland County

Route 637 north of Monterey

*Old General Store, New
Hampden, Highland County*

*Farm near headwaters of
the Middle River, Route 602,
Augusta County*

Sign, Route 637, New Hampden

Route 747 near 809,
Augusta County

Natural Chimneys, near Mount Solon, Augusta County. The seven formations range from 65 to 120 feet high; the age of the rock is estimated at 500 million years.

Hall of Fame Joust. Each year, modern-day combatants live out their medieval fantasies in this tournament at Natural Chimneys.

Valley Tour III

Go north on the Valley Pike, where at least one man has died for every yard over which the automobile travels. You may see the present only, yet the tread of the dead soldiers, blue and gray, still has the power to shake Valley hearts, and on this ground they can not be forgotten.

Here is New Market, where the bands played "Rockabye Baby" when the cadets marched in. Here are Endless Caverns. This is Mount Jackson, where Stonewall rested with his lemons and Bible. Five hundred Confederates lie in this burying ground, more than one of them unnamed and unknown. Nearby to the west, a former health spa with its large, rambling old wooden hotel, now operated as a church camp, is home to the Shenandoah Valley Music Festival, a summer-long celebration of the arts at Orkney Springs. And there is Woodstock, where Peter Muhlenberg threw off his pastor's robe to show a Confederate uniform.

In Edom, near the homestead where the Lincolns lived, practiced Dr. Joseph Bennett, who in 1794 performed a successful caesarean operation on his wife, saving both mother and child. Dr. Walter Reed, hero of yellow fever research, spent part of his youth in Harrisonburg. The law had its representatives in the Valley as well. In the high-ceilinged courthouse at Woodstock, the record books are full of the writings of Thomas Marshall, county clerk and father of Chief Justice John Marshall. Edmund Randolph, the nation's first attorney general, sleeps in the churchyard of the Old Chapel at Millwood.

The Inn at Narrow Passage,
Route 11 south of Woodstock,
Shenandoah County. The inn,
established in the 1740s, is
now a bed-and-breakfast.

Sevier House, New
Market, Shenandoah County.
John Sevier of New Market
moved west to become one
of the founders of Tennessee.

Vintage filling station, Mauzy,
Shenandoah County

Route 612,
Shenandoah County

Old schoolhouse, Route 701 at 717, Jerome, Shenandoah County

Fairfax Symphony Orchestra performing at the Shenandoah Valley Music Festival in Orkney Springs

*Orkney Springs Hotel,
Shenandoah County. Orkney
Springs is the home of the
Shenandoah Valley Music
Festival.*

A stretch of the Seven Bends of the North Fork, near Woodstock, viewed from a fire tower on Massanutten Mountain in Shenandoah County

Bryce Resort, a haven offering suburban amenities to well-to-do summer visitors to Shenandoah County

Through the middle Valley northward, where the Shenandoah bends seven times through black alluvial soil, Shenandoah County has a settled population, industrious and independent. Once it had a group of famous potteries. Samuel Bell set up his wheels in Strasburg in 1833. He was followed by sons and sons-in-law, all with an honest love of their craft, until there were six potteries in operation. The last wheel turned in 1908, and the craft has been abandoned. Here the North Fork of the Shenandoah bends east around the northern end of Massanutten to meet the South Fork at Front Royal.

The road leads through Middletown, site of the Cedar Creek battleground and Belle Grove, and on to Kernstown, where Jackson fought his first Sunday battle and suffered his first defeat. Along this stretch, Miss Charlotte Hillman dropped her tollgate in front of Sheridan and his whole army. The general humored her courage by paying for himself and staff, but told her that she would have to hold the United States Government accountable for the rest. And that is what she did. She counted the soldiers as they passed, presented her bill after the war, and collected.

Here on the gentle swells of land just south of Winchester, begins the lower Valley, home of the English settlers, a countryside of noble trees, old houses, long memories, and gentle manners. In Frederick and Clarke, Jefferson and Berkeley, the old houses tell the story, and it is not possible to escape their history.

On Cedar Creek stands Harmony Hall and its old mills. Here George Bowman sired four distinguished sons, one to be a colonel in the Revolution, two to go west with Lewis and Clark, one to command militia in Kentucky. A few miles northeast, Isaac Hite, grandson of the pioneer, built Belle

Victorian house, Hawkinsville, Shenandoah County

Spring Valley Farm, Route 42, Shenandoah County

Grove in 1787. Tradition says that Thomas Jefferson drew the plans. James and Dolley Madison stopped here on their honeymoon, for Mrs. Hite was Madison's sister. A little farther is the home of Joist Hite, Springdale.

Pages and Washingtons, Carters and Burwells, Randolphs, Peytons, Harrisons, Meades, Nelsons, Byrds, Pendletons, Lucases, Darks, seeded this ground. Pages or their descendants built Pagebrook and Annefield, where the box lilacs and syringa planted more than two hundred years ago by "sweet Anne Page" still grow and bloom. Pages came to own Dan Morgan's Saratoga. Pages built The Briars, where John Esten Cooke lived, wrote, and died.

Drive-in movie, Route 11
near Stephens City, Frederick
County

Opequon Presbyterian
Church after the blizzard
of March, 1993, Kernstown,
Frederick County

Old Town Mall, Winchester

A cousin of George Washington built old stone Fairfield. His brothers built Mordington and Harewood, the latter still in the hands of Washingtons today. Carter Hall attests the magnificence of Carter Burwell, who built it near Millwood in 1790. James Wood's Glen Burnie stands. At Greenway Court, there remains an office and the white post that Lord Fairfax set up.

These are but a few of the historic houses in the Valley. No list could cover them all; there are too many hidden away down curving lanes concealed by groves, retired behind long drives.

Winchester is not dreaming about its past. It is busy with its apple-storage warehouses, quick-freezing plants, plastic and auto-part manufacturing, medicinal and food-product plants. In the old portion of town, the tree-shaded streets frame gracious homes and lovely gardens. Winchester has a privately endowed public high school and a beautiful domed public library, the gift of Judge Handley, who came to the Valley and fell in love with it. Shenandoah College and Conservatory and the Patsy Cline

Route 600,
Frederick County

legacy are all part of Winchester, as is the Apple Blossom Festival held each spring, where Queen Shenandoah is crowned on the steps of Handley High School. Winchester and Berryville both feel they have a claim on the Byrds, Tom, Dick, and Harry. Admiral Richard Byrd reached both the North and South Poles. Tom avoided the limelight but in partnership with Harry made himself the largest apple grower in the world. Harry was governor of Virginia and a United States Senator.

The Berryville Pike leads on through Berryville, with Charles Town twelve miles beyond. On certain days Charles Town is crowded. But the visitors are not looking for the courthouse where John Brown was tried. They are on their way to the races at the track on the edge of town. Beyond Charles Town the highway dips and rises, for the mountains grow nearer, change from blue to green, from hazy smoothness to the shaggy reality of rocks and trees.

At the mouth of the Shenandoah River, where it joins the Potomac on its way to the Chesapeake, is Harpers Ferry. John Brown has not been forgotten in this town where he played out his fierce drama. One of the earliest colleges for black Americans, Storer, endowed by John Storer of Maine, stood here.

Jeff Miller, a recent graduate
of Shenandoah College and
Conservatory of Music,
Winchester

Handley High School,
Winchester. The public school
was endowed by Judge John
Handley, who lived in
Scranton, Pennsylvania,
but loved the Valley.

Long Branch Farms, Millwood,
Clarke County

Avenel, near Gaylord,
Clarke County

It is no longer in existence, its buildings taken over by the Department of the Interior, supervising the reconstruction of the Harpers Ferry National Monument. There is a plaque commemorative of Shepherd Haywood, the free man of color John Brown killed.

Rafters and tubers on the Shenandoah River near Harpers Ferry

In the spring of 1945, the Shenandoah Valley was threatened by a danger that would have made this the story of a nonexistent river, and of a Valley that would have partially vanished. In 1936 Congress authorized engineers to make plans for flood control along the Potomac and Shenandoah Rivers. After two years of study, they drew up a project for two dams on the Shenandoah. The rolling river would be converted into a lake fifty-two miles long and four miles wide. The people of the Valley rose to defend their land. With Senator Harry Byrd as their leader, they held mass meetings in every town to plan their protest. On April 3, a hearing was held in Washington. By noon of the next day, the Corps of Engineers announced that it would make an adverse report in the matter of the dams. And so a cloud rolled away from the Valley and the Shenandoah.

Epilogue

When Julia Davis' *The Shenandoah* was published in 1945, the Valley was still a relatively remote and isolated place. The Skyline Drive had offered its breathtaking vistas for nearly a decade, yet the Drive was itself not easily accessible, distant by a long day's journey on steep, winding roads from the population centers of Baltimore, Washington, and Richmond. The national interstate highway system was scarcely even a dream. The "daughter of the stars," if not solitary in her beauty, was at least sheltered.

Today the Shenandoah National Park is among the most visited of the nation's parks, the Skyline Drive on busy days resembling a 107-mile-long traffic jam. Activity has increased along the Valley floor as well, with the arrival of new people and new industry. As with all change, some of this is good, some bad. And as with everything else in the Valley, to sort out which is which requires knowledge not only of the present, but also of the past.

It can be argued that the Valley has never fully rebounded from the economic disasters of the Civil War and its aftermath. The land that Sheridan had laid waste recovered quickly, but other wounds were slower to heal. After the war, many of the middle class became impoverished, many of the poor became desperately so. The rich suffered too, with numerous long-established families losing their lands and possessions.

Pumpkin harvest, fall, Waynesboro

Slowly the Valley came back, depending as always on its fertile farmlands. By the 1890s apple orchards had become an economic mainstay, as did, later still, turkey raising. But neither of these pursuits was such as to create widespread prosperity, and when the Great Depression of the 1930s struck, it hit the Valley hard. At the same time, however, the depression opened a door to the future, for out of the economic ashes rose the Skyline Drive and Shenandoah National Park with their promise of an expanded tourist industry.

Tourism was nothing new to the Valley—even in the colonial days, visitors came to view the Natural Bridge and bask in the region's hot springs—but it had always been small in scale. The last decades of the nineteenth century brought a more substantial influx as wealthy city dwellers patronized spas and built summer homes in the cool mountains. In 1889 George Pollock established the Blue Ridge Park Association for the purpose of providing recreation for the well-to-do on his father's land, which had once been a mine site. Soon Washingtonians were flocking to the camp, at what is now Skyland, to climb Stony Man and escape the city's heat.

In 1924 Stephen Mather, the first director of the National Park Service, suggested opening a park in the Blue Ridge. The next year, Shenandoah National Park was commissioned. Commissioning it was

Highland County cattle roundup, conducted in the western manner by Mike Armstrong

Max and Wendal Smith
reaping dried corn for feed,
Route 11, Rockbridge County

Young cloggers carrying on a
folk tradition of the pioneers,
Bluegrass Festival, Skyline
Drive

Jay Eagles' Maple Sugar
Camp, Route 624 near Doe
Hill, Highland County. In spring,
the air is filled with the aroma
of the syrup cook-down.

Route 654, Doe Hill

Haying, Route 42
near Harrisonburg

Skyline Drive in the fall

one thing; creating it was another. One big obstacle was that most of the land was privately owned. Moreover, many of the inhabitants were mountain folk who had lived on the slopes and in the hollows of the Blue Ridge for generations, forming a subculture quite different from the one in the Valley. The mountaineers in their log cabins and homespun clothes had their own music, their own art, and their own dialect—some of their locutions harking back to Elizabethan England. Independent and proud, poor but self-subsistent, few of them wished to leave. Eventually, Virginia—which by agreement with Congress was to purchase the land for the park—passed a law that provided for buying the land and resettling

Foliage, Skyline Drive

the mountain people in the "interest of the public good." The United States Supreme Court upheld the legislation, and the mountaineers were removed, many finding new homes in the Valley. This controversial beginning for the new park kept the region in the public eye for many months.

Not until 1933 did the park begin to take its final shape. In that year President Franklin Roosevelt charged the newly-created Civilian Conservation Corps with building the Skyline Drive and retreeing the land. (Few people driving or hiking through the park realize that the lovely forests are relatively young; most of the land that makes up Shenandoah National Park had been clear-cut and cultivated by

1900.) At the same time, work was progressing rapidly on Benton MacKaye's inspiration, the Appalachian Trail, which follows the Blue Ridge as part of its 2,000-mile route from Maine to Georgia. Before long, too, the successful example of Shenandoah National Park had helped lead to the creation of the vast George Washington and Jefferson National Forests to the south and west. Later, Harpers Ferry National Historical Park capped the Valley's northern gateway. In the end, the parks, the national forests, and the Valley itself amounted to a single unique entity—a pastoral valley and tranquil river cradled within protected mountainscapes and abounding in historical relevance to some of the key themes of the American experience: Native American culture, European settlement, the Revolution, the Civil War, the Great Depression.

In 1956 President Dwight Eisenhower opened a new chapter in the Valley's history when he signed the legislation that authorized funding for the interstate highway system. The interstates changed the Valley forever. Until then, the pace of life in the Shenandoah had varied little over long decades. It was an easy, natural pace that turned with the seasons, the times for planting and harvesting. Even though World War II brought some industry to the region, the Valley remained largely rural and agricultural.

Route 637 near Monterey, Highland County

Skyline Drive

Nor had a slow, steady influx of outsiders over the years done much to alter the time-honored ways, for most of the newcomers were people who fitted seamlessly into the local pattern, buying old farms, belonging to one of the many churches ranging from Quaker and Mennonite to Baptist and Episcopal, and supporting the colleges and universities (there may be no other place where so small a population coincides with so many institutions of higher learning). Interstate 81 and, subsequently, I-66, I-70, and I-64 threatened to alter this pattern by opening the Valley to the outside world, bringing not only tourists but also industry and a new, twentieth-century wave of settlers, some of whom resided in the Shenandoah but commuted to work elsewhere.

Here is where questions of values arise. The Valley's high unemployment and weak economy make it vulnerable to choosing immediate gain over long-term benefit. This vulnerability is especially obvious in the lower Valley, where historic sites have sometimes been destroyed for new construction, often for industries that were unwelcome elsewhere; the same is true of several valuable natural sites along the Shenandoah River and the western flanks of the Valley. Too often, such planning as has existed has been local, makeshift, and piecemeal. What is needed, I believe, is a regional council that can address issues of development with an eye to the good of all residents and of the Valley itself. Since localities have been unable to formulate a general policy, it should be done at the state level.

Such a council should deal not only with industrial development, but also with tourism. Ironically, the Valley has not profited greatly from its attractiveness to outsiders. Tourism rides the mountain crest. Finding little in the way of housing or other amenities, visitors clamber in and out of caverns, cruise the Skyline Drive, visit the museums of Harpers Ferry, and climb back into their cars for the two-hour ride home. Some stay longer, to camp, hunt, or fish, to ride the river in canoes or the mountains on horseback. Yet when they leave, they know little of the Valley and its history. It is a paradox that an area with such unparalleled natural and historical endowments should have so weak and untapped a tourist economy.

We need a master plan, starting with an inventory of the Valley's resources—historical, natural, cultural, and educational as well as purely economic or industrial—and each item should be given its proper place in a value-oriented model. We are stewards of the Valley and of our heritage. Without care for both, our children will pay for our mistakes. The Valley itself tells us this.

Through it all, the Shenandoah River will follow its meandering course northward to the Potomac, the Blue Ridge will remain blue with the moisture of the lush Valley painting a soft pastel outline, Fort Valley will remain a private haven for the intrepid visitor as it lies hidden in the folds of the surrounding mountains, and the beautiful old chantey "Shenandoah" will continue to enthrall Americans everywhere with its simple, haunting melody.

Lucian Niemeyer

Index

Italicized page numbers refer to photographs and captions.